new
English

WITHDRAWN

new
English

book4

Maxwell Macmillan
International Publishing Group
New York   Oxford   Singapore   Sydney

Collier Macmillan Canada
Toronto

NEW ENGLISH 900

Project Editor: Peggy Intrator   **Contributing Editor:** Michael R. Lanzano

Senior Editor: Mary Ann Kingston Miller

Associate Editor: Gretchen Dowling

Consultant: Jean A. McConochie

Art Director: Zelda Haber

STAFF FOR STUDENT BOOK FOUR

Editor: Ellen Shaw

Editorial Assistant: Elyn Raymon

Illustrator: Erica Merkling

Art Editor: Anna Sabin

Production Supervisor: Gerald Vogt

PRINTING   8   9   10   11   YEAR   0   1   2   3

This is based upon
ENGLISH 900® copyright © 1964
Macmillan Publishing Co., Inc.

Philippines Copyright © 1978 MACMILLAN PUBLISHING CO., INC.

ISBN 0-02-974410-5

Collier Macmillan International, Inc.
866 Third Avenue, New York, New York 10022
Collier Macmillan Canada, Ltd.
Collier Macmillan Publishers
London

Printed in the United States of America

CONTENTS

Units 27, 28, 30-33 each contain two dialogue lessons. Units 29 and 34 contain three reading lessons each. The main grammatical points featured are listed below.

Introduction

The Story So Far

UNIT TWENTY-SEVEN   **THE PARTY**   **1**
                                 Reflexive pronouns
                                 Prepositions followed by gerunds
                                 Past habitual time with *used to*
                                 Time expressions *for* and *during*

UNIT TWENTY-EIGHT   **CONGRATULATIONS, PAULO!**   **14**
                                 Adverbs of manner
                                 Comparison of adverbs
                                 Too, enough, and *very*
                                 Adverbial clauses with *until*

UNIT TWENTY-NINE   **READING AND REFOCUS**   **30**
                                 MICHAEL'S BROTHER, GARY; AN APPLICATION TO COLLEGE; AT A COFFEE SHOP
                                 More on *used to*
                                 To want someone *to do* something
                                 Adverb review
                                 Various meanings of *get*
                                 Interested versus *interesting* (-ed v. -ing adjectives)

UNIT THIRTY   ASKING DIRECTIONS   52
             Modal: *should*
             The connector *so*
             The adverb *still*
             If + real conditional (with *will/won't*)

UNIT THIRTY-ONE   HOW MARTA MET MICHAEL 64
             As/while/when (interrupted action in
               the past)
             Even as an intensifier
             Hope
             So do I/Neither do I

UNIT THIRTY-TWO   O'NEILL'S COVER   76
             Gerunds
             Verbs followed by gerunds or infinitives
             How to

UNIT THIRTY-THREE THE RECONCILIATION 90
             The present perfect tense

UNIT THIRTY-FOUR   READING AND REFOCUS 106
             MICHAEL'S BLOCK; SERGEANT
              O'NEILL'S REPORT; JOE'S
             Articles *a/an, the*
             The hyphen
             More on adjective order
             Family relationships

BASE SENTENCE LISTING WITH INTONATION LINES 129

WORD INDEX   141

INTRODUCTION

Welcome to New English 900

In this introduction, we want to tell you something about the books you are going to be using.

1. What is New English 900?

NEW ENGLISH 900 is a six-level course for young adult students of English as a second language. It contains material from beginning to advanced levels of study. The series consists of six student textbooks, six workbooks, six teacher's books, and reel-to-reel or cassette recordings.

2. An Updated Program

This series is a revision of the original ENGLISH 900 which takes its name from the 900 Base Sentences presented in the six textbooks. These sentences cover the basic structures and basic vocabulary of the English language. The **Base Sentences** of NEW ENGLISH 900 always appear in a complete and authentic context. They are presented in dialogue form as spoken by a cast of fully-drawn characters who use the English language in a natural way to communicate their thoughts, ideas, and feelings.

3. How Your Textbooks Are Organized

There are 150 Base Sentences in each book, and they are numbered consecutively from Base Sentence 1, Book

1, Unit 1, through Base Sentence 900 in Book 6, Unit 50. New structures are introduced in Base Sentences, and these sentences provide "building blocks" for the rest of the materials studied in the series.

a. The Dialogue Unit

There are ten units in Book 1. Each unit consists of three lessons and contains fifteen Base Sentences. In Book 1, every lesson opens with a short **Dialogue** containing the Base Sentences. As you progress through the series, a continuous and integrated story will be unfolded through the dialogues and, later, the readings. (However, each textbook can be used separately). The dialogues are followed by **Substitution Drills** that introduce variations of the Base Sentences and provide the student with the pronunciation and drill material needed for mastery. The **Exercises** in each lesson can be used as oral and written drills. In addition, every unit contains a **Grammatical Preview,** a **Refocus (review) Exercise,** and a **Bonus Dialogue.**

b. Reading and Refocus Units

Beginning with Book 2, each text contains two **Reading and Refocus Units.** These units consist of thirty Base Sentences introduced in three **Reading Passages.** They are followed by **Comprehension Questions** and **Exercises** that review and contrast aspects of the language previously introduced.

c. Intonation and Word Index

Other features of each textbook include a complete listing of the Base Sentences introduced in that book. This listing appears with **Intonation Lines.** In addition, there is a **Word Index** that lists, in alphabetical order, all the new words in the book, and notes the unit, lesson, and sentence in which each word first appeared.

4. Your Workbooks and Tapes

A companion **Workbook** is available for each of the six textbooks. The Workbooks reinforce material from the text and develop pronunciation and writing skills. They are designed to be used both at home and in the classroom.

A series of **Pre-recorded Tapes** has been prepared for language laboratory use. These tapes include all material from the Dialogues, Substitution Drills, Readings, and Comprehension Questions in the Student Books, and from the Pronunciation Exercises in the Workbooks.

5. The Teacher's Books

The **Teacher's Books** are an integral part of NEW ENGLISH 900 . Organized to correspond to the student text, the Teacher's Book offers techniques and strategies of practical value to the teacher in the classroom. Included are suggested lesson plans, cultural notes, and a step-by-step outline of ways to present and practice the new material.

Our Thanks

Based on many suggestions we have received from you, the users, we offer NEW ENGLISH 900 . It represents a careful and extensive revision of the widely popular original series. In it, we hope to have combined the best of the old with the most exciting of the new.

THE STORY SO FAR

In the first three books, we established the characters and plot of *New English 900*. We met **Bill O'Neill,** an ice cream salesman at the World's Fair, and through him we met **Laura Segura,** a secretary, and her boss, **Mr. Crawford.** Laura was unhappy at her job, so she resigned. Mr. Crawford hired a new secretary, **Claire Lindstrom.** Mr. Crawford's son, **Michael,** is an artist.

Through Bill, we met **Paulo** and **Joana Farias,** and their mother. Paulo, a young businessman, is planning an art competition for the Brazilian Pavilion at the Fair. Joana is an art student. Their mother, **Alicia,** is visiting from Brazil. Joana Farias and Michael Crawford meet and begin to think about each other.

The Nikzad family is from Iran. We met **Simon Nikzad,** a banker at the Fair, his wife, **Zahra,** and their sons, **Ali** and **Hussein.** Ali is lively, independent, and stubborn.

The O'Neill family is American. We met Bill's wife, **Nora,** and their four children: **Billy** (Bill, Jr.), **Jack, Peggy,** and **Suzy.** Because the children are old enough to take care of themselves, Nora decides to take a job as a florist.

Miguel Morales and **Pedro Ortega** are friends. Miguel is a student visiting from Colombia. Pedro is a photographer and a ladies' man. Pedro and Miguel met the girl upstairs, **Marta Garcia.** To Pedro's surprise, Marta prefers Miguel. Miguel discovers that Pedro and Michael Crawford used to be good friends. They quarreled over a woman.

The Yamamotos own a store near the Fair. We met **Grandfather** and his grandson, **Jim.** We also get to know **Jim's mother and father.** Through the Yamamotos, we see the changing values of three generations.

These characters stay with the entire series and are the focus of our attention. An imaginary World's Fair provides a background for the series.

UNIT 27
THE PARTY

LESSON 1

450   MICHAEL: Good-bye, Miguel. Nice meeting you. Good-bye, Marta. Thanks for coming.

MARTA: Bye. Don't forget our English lesson on Wednesday.

MICHAEL: I won't. I'll be there. And why don't you come, too, Miguel?

MIGUEL: Thank you. I will. And thank you for inviting me to the party. It was a lot of fun.

MARTA: Thank you again, Michael. I'll see you next Wednesday. Joana, it was a pleasure meeting you.

JOANA: Thank you. It was a pleasure meeting you and Miguel.

ALL: Good night.

* * *

451 MICHAEL: Well. Let's sit down for a few minutes.
452   I can clean up later.

         JOANA: No, let me help you.

453 MICHAEL: No, that's all right. I can do it by myself in the morning. 453

454 JOANA: It was a very nice party. It's too bad Paulo had to work late.454

         MICHAEL: Yes, it is, but I'm glad you had a good time.

         JOANA: I liked your friends.

455/456 MICHAEL: They liked you, too. I could tell.455 As a matter of fact, you made everybody feel comfortable.456

         JOANA: That's easy. You're a great host.

457 MICHAEL: Well, you're a pretty good hostess. I was tired of giving parties by myself.457

GRAMMATICAL PREVIEW

Reflexive Pronouns

myself
yourself
himself/herself/itself
ourselves
yourselves
themselves

SUBSTITUTION DRILLS

1. Let's rest for **a few minutes.**
             a half an hour.
             awhile.
             fifteen or twenty minutes.
             a couple of hours.

2. I can **clean up**   later.
       make lunch
       do a wash
       make the beds
       dust
       vacuum the rugs

3. It's too bad Paulo **had to work late.**
                couldn't come.
                was so busy last night.
                fell asleep during the movie.

4. I love parties!   —I could **tell.**
                    see that.
                    guess.

5. You made everyone feel **comfortable.**
                                at home.
                                relaxed.
                                welcome.

6. I was tired of **giving parties**   by myself.
                        doing all the work
                        staying home every night
                        studying
                        travelling

7. I am **tired of** ·   living **by myself.**
        afraid of   alone.
        bored with
        excited about
        worried about

8. I **want**   to study by myself.
      have
      plan
      am trying

CONNECTED DRILLS

1.   I don't need help. **I**   can do it by **myself.**
                  You   You   yourself.
              You and I   We   ourselves.
          You and Michael   You   yourselves.
        Joana and Michael   They   themselves.
              Michael doesn't   He   himself.
                  Joana   She   herself.

2. I couldn't **speak English** when I **started school,** but I can now.
        cook   got married,
        change diapers   was single,
        type   graduated from high school,
        stay out late   lived with my parents,

EXERCISES

1. *For* answers the question "How long?"

Example: We talked *for a long time.*
                                        a few hours.

During answers the question "When?"

Example: I go to school *during the week.*
                                                    the summer.

Choose the right word for these sentences.

   a. Michael and Joana talked _____ a long time after the
        party.
   b. We hardly ever clean up our apartment _____ the week.
   c. While Gary was in college, he studied _____ five or six
        hours every day.
   d. It rained _____ the night. The streets are wet.
   e. Let's look around the store _____ a little while
        _____ our lunch hour.
   f. I usually go on vacation _____ six weeks _____
        the summer.

2. Change *alone* to "by ~self"

Example: Are you going to the party alone?
Are you going to the party by yourself?

a. Do you live alone?
b. Mr. Yamamoto prefers to work alone.
c. We couldn't lift those heavy boxes alone.
d. Suzy can't stay out late alone.
e. Did you and Gary plan your wedding alone?
f. Nora and Bill seldom have dinner alone.
g. I like to walk in the garden alone.
h. Ali would rather go to the Fair alone.

3. Answer the questions with "no." Follow the example.

Example: Did she go to the party with Pedro?
No. She went by herself.

a. Did Hussein do his homework with a classmate?
b. Did Marta and Miguel go to the movies with Pedro?
c. Did she live with other students when she studied in Madrid?
d. Did Ali go to the Fair with his father?
e. Did anyone help Michael serve the coffee?
f. Did anyone help you do your homework?

4. Choose the right form of the verb.
a. I'm afraid of _____ home by myself at midnight. (*walk, walking*)
b. Are we having spaghetti for dinner again? I'm tired of _____ the same thing three times a week. (*eat, eating*)
c. She doesn't want to _____ alone. (*live, living*)
d. I quit college because I was bored with _____ all the time. (*study, studying*)
e. Do you have to _____ tonight? (*study, studying*)

LESSON 2

458 JOANA: You know, when I was a teenager, I used to go to
459   parties all the time.**458** I enjoyed myself every
                   minute—parties, dances, boys.**459**

MICHAEL: It sounds like fun.

460 JOANA: It was. I used to live from dance to dance.**460**
461   On the weekends, Paulo and I never used to be
                   home.**461**

MICHAEL: Paulo? I don't believe it. I thought he worked all the
                   time—like my brother.

JOANA: Your brother? I didn't know you had a brother.

462 MICHAEL: It's a long story.

JOANA: We have time.

463 MICHAEL: O.K. How about a cup of coffee? Then I'll tell you
                   about myself.**463**

JOANA: Let me help.

464 MICHAEL: No. That's O.K. This kitchen is too small for two.**464**
465   Look around. Make yourself at home.**465**

GRAMMATICAL PREVIEW

I We You They He/She	used to	go	to Spain in the summer.

Affirmative Statement: She *used to* go to Spain in the summer.

Negative Statement: She *didn't use to* go to Spain in the summer.

Negative Question: *Didn't* she *use to* go to Spain in the summer?

Affirmative Question: *Did* she *use to* go to Spain in the summer?

Answers: 1. Yes, she *did.*
                       2. No, she *didn't.*

Tag Questions:

                    (+)   (−)
1. She used to go to Spain in the summer, didn't she?

                    (−)   (+)
2. She never used to go to Spain in the summer, did she?

SUBSTITUTION DRILLS

1. When I was a teenager, I used to **go to parties.**
                                       talk on the phone.
                                       listen to records.
                                       fight with my sister.

2. Paulo and I **never**   used to be home on weekends.
                  always
                  sometimes
                  often

3. I used to live from **dance to dance.**
                              meal to meal.
                              day to day.
                              minute to minute.

4. It's a **long**   story.
        true
        funny
        sad

5. I'll tell you about **myself.**
                my life.
                my past.
                my childhood.

6. Make yourself **at home.**
            comfortable.
            a drink.
            a sandwich.

7. I **enjoyed** myself.
    talked to
    cut
    hurt

CONNECTED DRILLS

1.
                          I enjoyed **myself**   at the party.
                    You   yourself
              Michael   himself
              Joana   herself
        Gary and I   ourselves
      You and Joana   yourselves
    The host and hostess   themselves

2.   I made **myself**   a drink.
    He   himself
    She   herself
    We   ourselves
    They   themselves

3. The **kitchen**   is too **small**   for **two people** to **cook in.**

house	big	one person	live in.
apartment	dark	my plants	grow in.
coffee	strong	me	drink.
food	spicy	us	eat.
movie	violent	children	watch.

EXERCISES

1. Fill in the reflexive pronoun.
   a.   She enjoyed _____ at the party.
   b.   He made _____ a drink.
   c.   Pedro bought _____ a car.
   d.   Mr. Farias taught _____ to drive.
   e.   I wrote _____ a note.
   f.   You taught _____ to swim, didn't you?

2. Add a reflexive pronoun for emphasis. It means "without any help from anyone."

   Example: Michael washed all the dishes.
   Michael washed all the dishes himself.

   a.   Henry edits the newsletter.
   b.   The children wrote to their grandmother.
   c.   My husband and I are building a house.
   d.   Claire must pay for law school.
   e.   I cleaned up the apartment.
   f.   The hostess planned the party.

3. What did you use to do when you were a child? Use these answers. Start each sentence with "When I was a child, . . ."

   Example: I visited my grandparents once a week.
   When I was a child, I used to visit my grandparents once a week.

   a.   I wore the same clothes as my brother.
   b.   I went to the country every summer.
   c.   I took dancing lessons.
   d.   I played all the time.
   e.   I worked in my father's store in the afternoon.
   f.   I loved to go to parties.

4. The lives of these people are different now. Follow the examples.

> **Examples:** 1. We seldom go to parties now. (*always*)
> *We always used to.*
>
> 2. Michael laughs a lot now. (*never*)
> *He never used to.*

a. Joana often wears blue jeans now. (*never*)
b. The Crawfords give many parties. (*seldom*)
c. I frequently go to see a movie in English. (*never*)
d. I usually finish my homework on time. (*rarely*)
e. Miguel always has a date on the weekend. (*seldom*)
f. Mr. Yamamoto sometimes takes a day off. (*never*)
g. Paulo hardly ever goes to parties. (*often*)

5. Combine the sentences.

> **Example:** This coffee is too strong. I can't drink it.
> *This coffee is too strong for me to drink.*

a. This book is too long. I can't read it this summer.
b. These shoes are too small. I can't wear them.
c. These problems are too difficult. The students can't do them.
d. That television program is too violent. The children mustn't
    watch it.
e. Those boxes are too heavy. Grandfather can't lift them.
f. Mexican food is too spicy. Mrs. Crawford can't eat it.

UNIT 28
Congratulations, Paulo!

LESSON 1

	PAULO:	Do you remember my idea for an art competition at the Fair?
466	JOANA:	Yes. How did they like it?
467/468	PAULO:	Very much. In fact, we're starting the project immediately.
469		And guess who's in charge?
	JOANA:	I don't know. I give up.
470	PAULO:	You give up too easily.**470** Your brother! Who else?
	JOANA:	Congratulations, Paulo! Now maybe you can take a few days off.
471		You work harder than anyone else in that office.**471**

PAULO: Joana, you don't take time off when you want a
promotion.

472 JOANA: You even eat more quickly than you used to.

PAULO: Hey, I didn't ask for a lecture!

JOANA: I'm sorry, Paulo. I think it's wonderful. Now tell me
about the competition. What are the rules? Can
Michael enter?

PAULO: Michael Crawford?

473 JOANA: Sure. He paints better th n anyone I know.₄₇₃ When
does the competition start?

GRAMMATICAL PREVIEW - ADVERBS OF MANNER

How does she sing? —She sings **beautifully.**

Beautifully is an adverb. It describes how she sings.

1. To make most adverbs, add "-ly" to an adjective: speak quiet*ly*, drive careful*ly*, sing beautiful*ly*, eat slow*ly*, come quick*ly*.*

2. A few words have the same adjective and adverb form. Here are some: *early, late, fast, hard, loud.* (*This is a hard test. He works hard.*) In comparisons, they have the same endings as adjectives:

He works harder than . . .
He works the hardest.

COMPARISON OF ADVERBS

	Comparative Degree	Superlative Degree
quick*ly*	*less/more* quick*ly than*	*the least/the most* quick*ly*
easi*ly*	*less/more* easi*ly than*	*the least/the most* easi*ly*

Irregular Forms

well	better than	the best
badly	worse than	the worst
much (a lot)	more than	the most
little	less than	the least

*Many English speakers leave off the "-ly" on one syllable adverbs; come *quick,* drive *slow.*

SUBSTITUTION DRILLS

1. How (much) did they like your idea?   —**Very much.**
—Not very much.
—A lot.
—They didn't.
—They weren't interested.

2.   **They liked it** very much.
I miss you
He needs me
Thank you
We love each other

3. We're starting the project **immediately.**
right away.
at once.
today.
right now.
as soon as possible.

4. You give up too **easily.**
quickly.
fast.
soon.
often.

5. You give up **more easily** than you used to.
more quickly
faster
sooner
more often

6. How does Paulo work? Does he work **hard?**
late?
efficiently?
carefully?
a lot?

7. Paulo **works harder**   than anyone I know.
      gets up earlier
      goes to bed later
      stays at work longer
      sleeps less
      works more

8. He **works the hardest**   of anyone I know.
      gets up the earliest
      goes to bed the latest
      stays at work the longest
      sleeps the least
      works the most

9. Michael **paints better**   than anyone I know.
       spells worse
       talks louder
       eats more slowly
       cleans less carefully
       changes jobs more frequently

10. Of all my friends, Michael **paints the best**.
                    spells the worst.
                    talks the loudest.
                    eats the most slowly.
                    cleans the least carefully.
                    changes jobs the most frequently.

CONNECTED DRILLS

1. Is Paulo a **hard worker?**   —Yes. He **works hard.**
    fast swimmer?   swims fast.
    careful driver?   drives carefully.
    conservative dresser?   dresses conservatively.
    good dancer?   dances well.
    bad singer?   sings badly.

2. Does Paulo **get up early?**   —Yes. He **gets up at six a.m.**
    go to bed late?   goes to bed at one a.m.
    write well?   writes excellent speeches.
    talk fast?   is sometimes hard to
           understand.

EXERCISES

1. Change the adjective to an adverb. Follow the example.

  Example: Michael is a ***good painter.***
      He paints well.

  a. Paulo is a **hard worker.**
  b. Billy and Jack are **fast swimmers.**
  c. Mr. Crawford is a **bad typist.**
  d. You and Joana are **good bakers.**
  e. Mr. O'Neill is a **careful driver.**
  f. Ali and I are **slow eaters.**
  g. Joana is a **good dresser.**
  h. Paulo is an **early riser.** (*gets up*)

2. Read this dialogue. Then answer the questions below.

A: Come on. I'll buy you an ice cream cone. What flavor would you like?

B: Strawberry's my favorite.

A: I don't think they have any strawberry. How about vanilla or chocolate?

B: I don't really like vanilla. I guess I'll have chocolate.

A: I'm just the opposite. I love vanilla, chocolate's okay, and I never have strawberry.

Questions:

a. Do A and B both like vanilla ice cream?

b. Which flavor does A like the most?

c. Does A like vanilla more than chocolate?

d. Does B like vanilla less than chocolate?

e. Which flavor does A like the least?

3. Make a comparison. Follow the examples.

Examples: 1. Laura dances well. Joana dances better.
Joana dances better than Laura.

2. Pedro lives simply. Michael lives even more simply.
Michael lives more simply than Pedro.

a. Joana cooks dinner often. Mrs. Farias cooks dinner even more often.

b. Mrs. Crawford gets up early. Mr. Crawford gets up even earlier.

c. I learn languages easily. My husband learns languages even more easily.

d. My father dresses conservatively. My uncle dresses even more conservatively.

e. Michael plays tennis badly. Gary plays tennis even worse.

f. You talk fast. I talk even faster.

g. Claire writes well. Henry writes even better.

4. Make a comparison. Follow the examples.

Examples: 1. Bill and Paulo work hard, but Mr. Crawford works even harder.
Mr. Crawford works the hardest.

2. Mr. and Mrs. Crawford dress conservatively, but Mr. Nikzad dresses even more conservatively.
Mr. Nikzad dresses the most conservatively.

a. Mrs. Nikzad and Hussein eat slowly, but Ali eats even more slowly.
b. Mr. Crawford and Pedro get angry easily, but Mr. Nikzad gets angry even more easily.
c. Michael and Miguel dance badly, but Marta dances even worse.
d. The two brothers write home frequently, but their sister writes home even more frequently.
e. Bill and Nora don't go out often, but Miguel goes out even less often.
f. Pedro and Paulo dance well, but Joana dances even better.

LESSON 2

474   PAULO: We won't announce the contest until Mr. Crawford finishes the brochure.

JOANA: Oh, is he doing the brochure for you?

PAULO: Yes.

JOANA: What does his office look like?

475/476   PAULO: It's large enough, and modern and businesslike.**475** And very formal—too formal, perhaps.**476** Why do you ask?

JOANA: Just curious. I'm trying to imagine Michael in that office.

PAULO: What do you mean?

477   JOANA: Michael gave himself a deadline. Either he does well this year, or he gives up art and goes into business with his father.**477**

478/479   PAULO: How well is "well"? How is he going to measure
480   success? Does he have to paint as well as the masters?

JOANA: I don't really know. But he has to prove something to himself.

PAULO: Then this competition could be his *chance.

JOANA: Yes, it could.

*chance here means "opportunity"

GRAMMATICAL PREVIEW

UNTIL

1. In affirmative sentences, *until* indicates a specific time *at the end* of a period.

Examples: 1. He played baseball *until* 5:00.
(*He stopped at 5:00.*)

2. I'm going to work for Mr. Crawford *until* I find another job. (*When I find another job, I'll quit.*)

2. In negative sentences, *until* indicates a specific time *at the beginning* of a period. The meaning isn't really negative.

Examples: 1. He didn't get married *until* he was fifty years old. (*He got married when he was fifty.*)

2. I won't leave *until* you answer my question. (*I'll leave when you answer my question.*)

SUBSTITUTION DRILLS

1. We won't announce
the contest until **Mr. Crawford finishes the brochure.**
we find the right exhibition area.
we know the cost.
my boss chooses the judges.

2. Joana **studied art**   until she came to New York.
went out a lot
had short hair
worked in a boutique

3. His office looks very **modern and businesslike.**
formal and busy.
spacious and pleasant.
big and comfortable.
light and airy.

4. Michael gave himself a **deadline.**
test.
trip around the world.
party.

5. He wants to paint as **well**   as the masters.
creatively
beautifully
successfully
much

6. I'll call as **soon**   as I can.
often
early
many times

7. How did Mr. Crawford end his meeting? —**By saying good-bye.**
—With a handshake.
—Politely.

8. How did Paulo contact Mr. Crawford? —By **letter.**
phone.
telegram.
mail.

CONNECTED DRILLS

1. His office is *too* **formal. I felt uncomfortable there.**
casual.   It wasn't businesslike enough.
noisy.   I couldn't hear myself think.
cold.   There's never any heat.

2. His office   is **large**
   Michael   young
   Paulo   smart
   Mr. Crawford   rich

   enough to be impressive.
              enter the contest.
              be vice president.
              take us all to dinner!

3. His office is **large**
   This library   quiet
   This shelf   low
   This suit   formal

   enough for twenty people *to* **fit in.**
              me *to* study in.
              Ali *to* reach.
              Paulo *to* wear to the party.

4. How **well**   is **"well"?**
      formal   "formal"?
      perfect   "perfect"?
      final   "final"?
      fast   "fast"?

5. How **well**   does he **paint?**
    fast   type?
    loudly   speak?
    quickly   drive?
    often   write home?
    well   do in school?

6. How is he going to **measure success?**
                    finish in time?
                    buy a sports car?
                    find an apartment?
                    lose weight?

    —By **winning the contest.**
        painting every day.
        borrowing some money.
        looking in the paper.
        not eating candy.

EXERCISES

1. Write a negative sentence for each situation with "until."

Example: We will announce the contest when Mr. Crawford
        finishes the brochure.
        *We won't announce the contest until Mr. Crawford
        finishes the brochure.*

a.   We bought a house when we got married.
b.   We'll start dinner when Claire arrives.
c.   I will eat when I get hungry.
d.   I will leave when you answer my question.
e.   Mr. Crawford will finish the brochure when he has all the
     information.
f.   Michael will be happy when he wins the competition.

2. Look at this information:
Hussein, Linda, and Tom played tennis last Saturday. They played five games. Hussein won five games. Tom didn't win any. Linda won four games.

Now answer these questions:
  a. Who played the best of the three?
  b. Who played the worst?
  c. Did Linda play better than Tom?
  d. Did Tom play worse than Hussein?
  e. Did Hussein play well?
  f. Did Tom play as well as Linda?
  g. Did Linda play as badly as Tom?

3. Look at this information:
Laura types sixty words a minute. Paulo types seventy words a minute. Claire types seventy-five words a minute.
  a. Of the three, who types the most quickly?
  b. Who types the most slowly?
  c. Does Paulo type more quickly than Claire?
  d. Does Claire type less quickly than Laura?
  e. Does Laura type as quickly as Claire?

4. Answer the questions. Follow the example.

> **Example:** How is Michael going to measure success? (*win the contest*)
> *By winning the contest.*

    a. How did you learn to cook so well? (*watch a famous chef on T.V.*)
    b. How can I find a job? (*go to an employment agency*)
    c. How did he get here so fast? (*run*)
    d. How are they going to buy a house? (*borrow money from the bank*)
    e. How can Claire please Mr. Crawford? (*come in on time*)

5. Answer the questions. Follow the example.

> **Example:** How did Paulo contact Mr. Crawford? (*letter*)
> *By letter.*

    a. How do you pay your bills? (*check*)
    b. How did Joana and Paulo come to the United States? (*plane*)
    c. How are you and Bill going to the airport? (*taxi*)
    d. How did she make her wedding dress? (*hand*)
    e. How did you order the flowers? (*phone*)

6. Answer the questions. Follow the example.

> **Example:** How did you open the door? (*key*)
> *With a key.*

    a. How did he do his homework? (*dictionary*)
    b. How did he do the math problems? (*calculator*)
    c. How did you paint your apartment? (*three brushes*)
    d. How did she thank the Crawfords? (*note*)
    e. How did you cool the apartment so quickly? (*air conditioner*)

7. Use "too" or "enough"

Example: Why are you moving?
—Because my apartment is _____ noisy (to sleep in). Also, it's not big _____.
Because my apartment is too noisy (to sleep in). Also, it's not big enough.

a. Why can't I enter the competition?
—Because you're _____ old (to enter). The age limit is forty.

b. Why can't Ali go to the Fair by himself?
—Because he's not old _____.

c. Why wasn't Mr. Crawford happy with Laura?
—Because she wasn't efficient _____.

d. Why didn't Laura like Mr. Crawford?
—She thought he was _____businesslike—inhuman, as a matter of fact.

e. Tell me about Mr. Crawford.
—He's very formal. Some people are not comfortable with him. They think he's _____ formal.

f. Tell me about Paulo.
—He works very hard. Joana worries about him. She thinks he works _____ hard and needs to relax.

g. Tell me about Michael.
—He works very hard, too. But his father doesn't think painting is serious work. He thinks Michael isn't serious _____ about his future.

UNIT 29
Reading and Refocus

LESSON 1

Michael's Brother, Gary

[*After the party, Michael tells Joana about his brother.*]

481   Gary, my brother. Gary Whitney Crawford, Jr. He looks
482   just like me, *you know, Joana.**481** At least he used to.**482**
483   He's eighteen months older than I am, but as kids we used to
       wear the same clothes and pretend we were twins!**483** Gary
       was the greatest brother in the world, and in many ways, he
484   was my father, too. Dad didn't have time for me. He was too
       busy.**484**
485   Gary and I went to the same college, but that's when
       things started to change.**485** He studied business. Why did he

*You know is a very common expression. English speakers often use it to ask a listener
  "Are you paying attention?" or "Do you understand me?" A listener usually says
  uh-huh to show he's listening.

486   study business? Because my father wanted him to.**486** He
used to study night and day. I studied art and worked hard at
487   it. But I had time for my friends, too. Gary and I saw each
other less and less.**487**

488   When Gary graduated, he went to work for my father.**488**
He stayed at the office until late at night. He kept to himself
489   a lot. Like my father, Gary was always busy.**489**

     Then one night, Gary and my father had a terrible fight.
The next morning Gary moved out. We never saw him again.

     About a year ago, a college friend of mine saw Gary in
London. He was with a woman and a baby. My friend was
490   sure it was Gary. He never forgets a face.**490**

QUESTIONS ABOUT "MICHAEL'S BROTHER, GARY"

Fact:
The answers are *clear* in the story.

1. Which brother is older, Gary or Michael?
2. Did Gary and Michael use to look like each other?
3. Did Michael and Gary go to different colleges?
4. In college, did Gary study all the time, or did he spend some time with friends?
5. Was Gary closer or less close to Michael after he graduated?
6. Where did Michael's friend see Gary?

Inference:
You can *guess the right answers* from the story.

1. Did Gary and Michael use to think like each other when they were young?
2. In college, was Gary more like his father or Michael?
3. Does Michael think Gary wanted to study business?
4. Why did Michael want to go to the same college as Gary?
5. Why did Gary leave home?
6. Does Michael understand why Gary left home?

To the Student:
There are *no wrong answers* to these questions.

1. In the United States, you go to college when you finish secondary school. Do you have colleges in your city? What kind of degree can you get in college?
2. What did you study in college or in school?
3. Is it necessary to have a college education in order to get a good job in your country?
4. Do you want your children to have the same job as you do, or do you want them to have different jobs?
5. Do you think Mr. Crawford studied art in school, or did he study business?
6. What does "never forget a face" mean?

USING YOUR ENGLISH

I. WANT SOMEONE TO DO SOMETHING

A. "Gary studied business because my father wanted him to (study business)."

In the reading, the sentence above means: (choose one)
1. Gary studied business because he wanted to.
2. Gary studied business because his father thought it was a good idea.

The correct answer is (2). We don't know if Gary wanted to study business. The sentence itself does not tell us what Gary wanted. It tells us what his father wanted.

B. Here are ten things Michael wants to do.
1. He wants to be a painter.
2. He wants to travel.
3. He wants to speak with his brother.
4. He wants to buy a new car.
5. He wants to stay in his apartment on 88th Street.
6. He wants to study Portuguese.
7. He wants to invite his friends for dinner.
8. He wants to have another party.
9. He wants to send his mother flowers for her birthday.
10. He wants to work in a museum.

Michael's father doesn't want him to do any of these things. Change the sentences.

Example: 1. *Mr. Crawford doesn't want Michael to be a painter.*

II. TOO and VERY

A. 1. *Very + adjective* intensifies the adjective. It makes the meaning stronger.

   Examples: a. *She works very hard.*
   b. *He is very handsome.*

   2. *Too + adjective* also makes the meaning stronger, but it usually indicates some kind of negative opinion or judgment. *Too* indicates excess.

   Examples: a. I can't study. *It's too hot.* (to study)
   b. I can't sleep. *I'm too nervous.* (to sleep)
   c. You look tired. *You work too hard.*

B. Use *too* or *very* in the sentences below.

   1. He talks _____ fast. It's fun to listen to him.
   2. He talks _____ fast. I can't understand him.
   3. It's _____ sunny today. It's a perfect day for the beach.
   4. It's _____ sunny today. I'm getting a headache from the sun.
   5. This coffee is _____ strong. I can't drink it this way.
   6. I like _____ strong coffee. I use three spoons of coffee for every cup of water.
   7. The movie began at 9:00, and it's 9:15 now. It's _____ late to go.
   8. It's _____ late, but let's go to the movies. I don't have to get up until 10:00 tomorrow morning.
   9. The suitcase is _____ heavy, but he's used to carrying heavy things.
   10. The suitcase is _____ heavy. I can't lift it by myself.

III. AS

A. "As kids we used to wear the same clothes."
In the sentence above, *as kids* means "when we were kids."

B. Follow the pattern. Rewrite the sentences below.
Begin each one with the word *as*.

1. When I was a child, I was very poor.
2. When he was a soldier, he slept in the mud.
3. When she was a teacher in Africa, she met many interesting people.
4. When I was a student, I was much more serious than I am now.
5. When he was a young man, he didn't have much money.

IV. LIKE

A. *Like my father, Gary was always busy* means "My father was always busy. Gary was, too."

B. Join these sentences in the same way. Follow the example above.

1. My mother likes to work in the garden. I do, too.
2. The oceans are slowly becoming polluted. The rivers and the lakes are, too.
3. Joana's father likes music very much. Joana does, too.
4. Japan is worried about industrial pollution. Many other countries are, too.
5. Thailand grows rice. China does, too.

LESSON 2

An Application to College
Part X: *The Essay*

Write an essay of 200-500 words. You may choose any topic for your essay.

491
492/493

494

I would like to write about two people, a man and a woman.**491** They live quiet lives.**492** When they go out into the street, no one asks for their autographs, but everyone in their profession knows and respects them.**493** They work as a team.**494** The woman is a journalist. The man is a photographer.

495

496

They met on their first job.**495** They both worked for a famous picture magazine. She wrote the articles, and he took the photographs. The magazine sent them all over the world *to cover important events.**496** They won many awards and medals.

497/498

499

One day the magazine **went bankrupt.**497** Many other magazines and newspapers offered them positions, but at this point the man and the woman decided to work independently.**498** She decided she wanted to write a book about her experiences at the magazine. He wanted to work on a photographic essay on ***bonsai.**499**

500

For once, they did not worry about deadlines and editors.**500** They enjoyed their work and grew professionally. Their books were successful. When they finished their separate projects, they decided to work as a team again.

Now they are ready to go, day or night, on a moment's notice. When there are earthquakes in Honduras, they are there. When there are battles in the Middle East, they are there. When there are local tragedies, they are there, too.

My parents are a great team.

James Yamamoto

*to cover means "to write about"
**to go bankrupt means "to lose all your money"
***bonsai is the Japanese art of growing miniature trees and shrubs.

Questions about "An Application to College"

Fact:
The answers are *clear* in the story.

1. Who wrote this essay?
2. What do Jim's parents do for a living?
3. Do people in their professions respect them?
4. Did Mr. and Mrs. Yamamoto know each other as children?
5. Did the magazine fire them, or did it lose all its money?
6. Did Jim write this essay for a magazine or for a college application?

Inference:
You can *guess the right answers* from the story.

1. Who chose the topic for this essay, Jim or the college?
2. What does Jim mean when he says, "They live quiet lives"?
3. Are Mr. and Mrs. Yamamoto good at their jobs?
4. Do the Yamamotos like their work, or do they do it just because of the money?
5. Why did the Yamamotos decide to work independently for awhile?
6. Do the Yamamotos travel a lot?

To the Student:
There are *no wrong answers* to these questions.

1. Do you read a lot? Which do you prefer, magazines or books?
2. Is there a famous picture magazine in your country? What is it called? What kind of events does it cover?
3. Do you know any husband and wife teams?
4. What could be the best thing about working with one's husband or wife?
   What could be the worst?
5. In your country, would a team like the Yamamotos work out or not?
6. *Jim* is the nickname (short form) of *James*. Do you know what the nickname for *William* is? (It's one of the characters in the book.)

THINKING ABOUT ADVERBS

A. These words and phrases all answer a HOW question.

with a key • by car • with scissors and tape •
with kindness • in a kind way • on a typewriter •
with help • in a confident way • by hand • quickly •
kindly • on foot • carefully • easily • slowly •
with care • in a careful way • with hard work •
with his foot • by bus • confidently • with an old knife •
quietly • with confidence

1. Divide the words and phrases into four different kinds.

HOW # 1	HOW # 2	HOW # 3	HOW # 4
a. *quickly*	a. *by car*	a. *with a key*	a. *with kindness*
b. *kindly*	b. _____	b. _____	b. *in a kind way*
c. _____	c. _____	c. _____	c. _____
d. _____	d. _____	d. _____	d. _____
e. _____		e. _____	e. _____
f. _____			f. _____
g. _____			g. _____
			h. _____

2. Some of the words in Group # 1 mean the same as the phrases in Group # 4. Which ones?

Example: *kindly* = with kindness = in a kind way

What about these words? How else would you express their meaning?
   a. *intelligently* =
   b. *angrily* =
   c. *lovingly* =
   d. *beautifully* =

3. Fill in the sentences below with suitable HOW adverbials.

Choose them from the list on page 39. There is more than one correct
answer. As you will see, you can always put the HOW # 1 adverbs
after the verb and object. You can sometimes put them before the
verb and sometimes before the subject.

Example: Ali's teacher spoke # 1 to him.
              kindly, slowly, quietly, etc.

a.   Ali's teacher spoke to him # 1.
b.   Ali's teacher told him a story # 1.
c.   Ali's teacher # 1 told him a story.
d.   Ali's teacher # 1 told him to behave.
e.   I started the car # 3.
f.   I started the car # 1 # 3.
g.   Tom kicked the ball # 3.
h.   Tom kicked the ball # 1 # 3.
i.   Tom # 1 kicked the ball # 3.
j.   Bill goes to work # 2.
k.   Bill goes to work # 1 # 2.
l.   Jack made his mother a present # 2.
m.   Jack made his mother a present # 2 # 3.
n.   Jack # 1 made his mother a present # 2 # 3.
o.   Nora arranged the flowers # 1 # 4.
p.   The student answered the question # 4.
q.   The student answered the question # 1.
r.   The student # 1 answered the question.

4. Some of the sentences below are correct and some are incorrect. Mark the correct ones *okay* and change the incorrect ones.

> **Examples:** 1. She **with care** picked up the package.
> *She picked up the package with care.*
>
> 2. She **carefully** picked up the package.
> *okay*

a. He **with a key, easily** opened the door.
b. He **slowly** opened the door.
c. He opened **quickly** the door.
d. He spoke **quickly** to the salesman.
e. The magazine grew **with hard work rapidly.**
f. The salesman looked at the customer **carefully.**
g. The salesman looked **carefully** at the customer.
h. The salesman watched **carefully** the customer.

B. 1. These words and phrases are all adverbials.
They tell you HOW, WHEN, or WHERE about the verb.

quietly • carefully • by hand • usually • early •
beautifully • hard • yesterday • recently •
at the office • over there • late • by boat • all day •
well • last week • to the concert • here •
with a calculator • on (with) the typewriter • quickly •
right before class • in class •

2. Put the adverbials above next to the right question word.

HOW: *quietly, with a calculator,* _____, _____,

_____, _____, _____,

_____, _____, _____.

WHEN: *recently,* _____, _____, _____,

_____, _____, _____,

_____

WHERE: *to the concert,* _____, _____,

_____, _____

3. This is the usual order for adverbials in sentences.

I did my homework
HOW #1   WHERE   HOW #3   WHEN
quickly in my office on the typewriter right before class.

Arrange these groups of words into sentences.

1. quickly
    around the park
    he runs
    every morning

2. the baby wrote
    yesterday
    with a big black pencil
    all over the walls

3. on the farm
    hard
    they worked
    all their lives

4. last night
    she sang
    at the concert
    beautifully

5. alone
    Ali watched T.V.
    in his room
    before dinner

6. Bill, Jr. made Nora a present
    in class
    last week
    by hand

LESSON 3

At a Coffee Shop

Look at all those people. They all have good jobs and houses in the country. O.K., maybe all of them don't have houses in the country, but they probably have more than **501** you. Laura, stop it. Don't feel so sorry for yourself.₅₀₁ **502** Nobody likes to get out and look for a job.₅₀₂ **503/504** I'm getting depressed again.₅₀₃ It's time for a change.₅₀₄ Maybe I'll meet someone in an elevator, and he'll offer me a wonderful job. My worries will be over. Stop it, Laura. Be realistic.

505   Yes. It's time for a change. I hate offices. I don't hate work
             — that's why I got the job with Crawford — but I don't like
506   offices.₅₀₅ I don't feel human in an office. I'd rather work
507   with people than with files and typewriters.₅₀₆ But how? I
             could be a real estate agent, a travel agent, a . . . anything,
             as long as it isn't boring.₅₀₇

             Claire's going to law school. Crawford's son, what's his
             name? . . . Michael. Yes. He wants to be an artist. Henry
             Leeds likes his job. He doesn't want to do anything else. It *is*
             possible to be happy at your job.

508   I could teach Spanish. No. I don't have the patience. I
             think I'd like to be my own boss.₅₀₈ I like to sew. Maybe I
             could open a small dress shop. I wonder how much you
             need to start a shop.

509   My head is spinning. I must be getting hungry.₅₀₉ I'm tired,
510   too. Maybe I'm getting a cold.₅₁₀ No. You're not getting a
             cold. You're just depressed. And scared. A dress shop. I'll
             have to think about that.

             WAITER: Would you like to order now?

Questions about "At a Coffee Shop"

Fact:
The answers are *clear* in the story.

1. Who is thinking in the story?
2. Who is Laura talking to in the story?
3. Does Laura want to get another office job?
4. Does she know what kind of job she wants?
5. Does she want an easy job or a job she cares about?
6. Is Laura really getting a cold, or is she just tired?

Inference:
You can *guess the right answers* from the story.

1. Would Laura rather be an accountant than a secretary?
2. Does she know what she wants to be, or is she trying to find out what she wants to be?
3. Does she want to change jobs or careers?
4. Is Laura scared of responsibility?
5. Why is she depressed?
6. How does she feel about looking for a job?

To the Student:
There are *no wrong answers* to these questions.

1. Do people often change jobs in your country?
2. Do you know anyone who changed careers after the age of thirty-five?
3. Do you think Laura's lucky to be single, with no family responsibilities, or does it make everything harder?
4. Would you rather be your own boss or work for someone else?
5. How did you get your job?
6. What do you think is important in one's work — security, independence, happiness, money, reputation, responsibility . . . what?

USING YOUR ENGLISH

GET

A. The verb *get* (past tense - *got*) has many meanings.

Examples: 1. Laura wants to *get* a new job.   OBTAIN
She's *getting* a cold.

2. She's *getting* depressed.   BECOME or GROW

3. She *got* her last pay check yesterday.   RECEIVE

4. She's going to *get* home late tonight.   ARRIVE

B. Fill in the blanks with the correct form of *get*, and write the meaning next to the sentence.

Examples: Where did you *get* that blouse? I love it!   *OBTAIN*
—I *got* it at a little shop downtown.   *OBTAIN*

1. How did you _____ so wet?
—I was standing on the corner, and a bus splashed me.
2. I quit my job. I _____ tired of typing all day long.
3. Did I _____ any mail?
—Yes. You _____ a couple of letters.
4. While you're in the kitchen, could you _____ me a glass of water?
5. Guess what! I _____ a raise!
6. The class wasn't interesting. After the first session, it _____ boring.
7. It's _____ late. We have to leave.

8. I'm hungry, aren't you? Let's stop at the coffee shop and
   _____ something to eat.
9. We _____ to the theater late and missed the first act.
10. I can't _____ to the post office before it closes.
11. I _____ a calculator for my birthday.
12. She _____ a phone call from her mother in Paris.
13. Let me see . . . did I _____ everything? Bread, milk,
    sugar, butter . . . Oh, I forgot to _____ coffee.
14. Where's Henry? He was here this morning.
    —He _____ sick and went home.
15. I found three gray hairs this morning. I guess I'm _____
    old.

C. This chart shows what Alice does in the morning every day.

ALICE'S MORNING SCHEDULE

7:00	get up
7:15	get into the shower
7:30	get dressed
7:45	get breakfast
8:00	get out of the house
8:10	get a newspaper
8:15	get on the bus
8:45	get off the bus
9:00	get to her desk at the bank

Answer the questions about Alice's schedule. Use the correct
form of *get* .
  1. What does she do at 7:00 every day?
  2. What did she do at 7:00 yesterday?
  3. It's 7:00. What's she doing now?
  4. What does she do at 7:30 every day?
  5. It's 9:00. What's she doing now?
  6. What did she do at 8:45 yesterday?
  7. What did she do at 7:15 yesterday?
  8. What does she do at 9:00 every day?
  9. It's 7:15. What's she doing now?
 10. What did she do at 7:30 yesterday?
 11. What does she do every day at 8:15?
 12. It's 8:45. What's she doing now?
 13. What does she do at 8:10 every day?
 14. What did she do at 8:00 yesterday?
 15. It's 8:10. What's she doing now?

D. Here are ten different uses of *get*.

get on (a bus)	ENTER
get in (a car)	ENTER
get off (a bus)	LEAVE
get out of (doing something)	AVOID, ESCAPE
get up (from your seat)	ARISE
get up (at 9:00)	WAKE UP
get to (a place)	REACH, GO
get away	LEAVE, ESCAPE
get through	REACH
get	UNDERSTAND, CATCH (informal)

Complete the sentences. Use the right idiomatic expression and the correct form of *get*.

Examples: Could you tell me how to *get to* the Fair?
—Take the No. 3 bus and *get off* at the last stop.
Then take the No. 2. Be sure you *get on* the No. 2 because all the other buses go downtown.

1. I don't _____ what you mean. Can you explain it again, please?
2. Mr. Crawford usually _____ at 6:30 in the morning. He's an early riser.
3. You were at the lake this weekend, weren't you? Did you _____ any fish?
   —Well, I _____ a big one, but he _____.
4. What time do you usually _____ work?
5. I'm trying to call Nancy, but her phone is busy. I can't _____.
6. The teacher tried to explain, but the students just didn't _____ it.
7. Some students try to _____ doing their homework.
8. Many children try to _____ eating vegetables. They don't like the taste.
9. This trip is awfully long. I don't think we'll ever _____ the end of it.
10. How do you like my new car? _____ and I'll give you a ride.
11. It's late, and you're in bed. Are you ever going to _____?
12. When you meet an older person, it's polite to _____ from your seat.
13. I'm so tired, but I can't _____ sleep.
14. Are you ever going to _____ the phone? I'm waiting for an important call, and he won't be able to _____.

UNIT 30
Asking Directions

LESSON 1

511   MR. YAMAMOTO: Excuse me, sir. Can you tell me where the
Japanese Garden is?511

512   BILL: It's quite a long walk from here.512 Why

513   don't you take the Fair bus? It stops right
over there, in the Plaza of Nations.513

514   Between the statue and the fountain.514

      MR. YAMAMOTO: The statue? Excuse me, I don't see as well as
I used to.

      ALI: Hi, Mr. O'Neill.

515   BILL: Oh, hi, Ali. Would you do me a favor?

       ALI: Sure.

516   BILL: Would you take this gentleman to the bus stop over there?

       ALI: Sure. [*to Mr. Yamamoto*] Hi. Where do you want to go?

      BILL: The gentleman wants to go to the bus stop, Ali.

       ALI: [*to Mr. Yamamoto*] But where are you going after that?

      BILL: He asks a lot of questions.

517   ALI: My father says I shouldn't ask so many questions. He
518   says it's not polite. So I'm sorry.₅₁₈ But I still want to
519   know.₅₁₉

GRAMMATICAL PREVIEW

SHOULD

Subject Pronoun	Modal	Verb	
I You We They He/She/It	(+) should (−) shouldn't	take	the Fair bus.

Affirmative Statement: He *should* take the Fair bus.

Negative Statement: He *shouldn't* take the Fair bus.

Negative Question: *Shouldn't* he take the Fair bus?

Affirmative Question: *Should* he take the Fair bus?

Answers: 1. Yes, he *should*. 2. No, he *shouldn't*.

Tag Questions:

1. He should take the Fair bus, shouldn't he?

2. He shouldn't take the Fair bus, should he?

SUBSTITUTION DRILLS

1. It's too far to walk to the Plaza of Nations.

> **You** should take the Fair bus.
> We
> They
> He

2. Should   I get off the bus at the next stop?
   Shouldn't

3. My father says I shouldn't **ask so many questions.**
   tell so many lies.
   eat so much ice cream.
   waste so much time.
   spend so much money.

4. Would you **do me a favor?**
   do something for me?
   give me a hand?
   help me out?

5. Would you **take this gentleman to the bus stop?**
   Could   help this woman cross the street?
   show these people the way to the Japanese Garden?
   bring back some coffee for me?
   mail a letter for me?

6. Can you tell me where **the Japanese Garden**   **is?**
   the Plaza of Nations
   the bus stop
   the nearest subway station
   Main Street

7. It's **quite a long walk**   from here.
   pretty far
   about five blocks away
   not easy to get to

8. The Fair bus stops
      right over there, **in the Plaza of Nations.**
           between the statue and the fountain.
           in front of the embassy.
           on the corner.
           directly opposite the Japanese Garden.

9. Are you still **here?**   It's 2:30 in the morning!
         up?
         working?
         doing your homework?

CONNECTED DRILLS

1. It's not **polite to ask a lot of questions.**
      safe to walk in the park at night.
      easy to find a job in this town.
      too late to change your mind.
      time to leave.

      So **I'm sorry.**
         be careful.
         don't give up yet.
         think it over a little more.
         be patient.

2. I know I shouldn't **ask so many questions,**
         be late for work,
         worry about you,
         gain any more weight,

      but I still **want to know where you're going.**
         need eight hours of sleep at night.
         get scared when you're out late.
         love to eat dessert.

EXERCISES

1.   Restate these sentences. Change "should" to "shouldn't."

Example: Children should be polite. (*impolite*)
Children shouldn't be impolite.

a.   You and Billy should drive slowly. (*so fast*)
b.   A library should be a quiet place. (*noisy*)
c.   Mr. Crawford should be more understanding. (*so critical*)
d.   Laura should save money. (*spend so much money*)
e.   You and I should go to bed early. (*stay up so late*)
f.   I should stay home. (*go out so often*)

2. Say what someone *should do* in these situations.

Example: I'm too tired to walk home tonight.
You should take a bus.

a.   I went to a dinner party at the Crawfords'. (*write a thank-you note to Mrs. Crawford*)
b.   Laura doesn't like to live by herself. (*find a roommate*)
c.   Ali and Hussein are crossing a busy street. (*be careful*)
d.   Michael's apartment is a mess. His mother is coming to visit him. (*clean it up*)
e.   Maria and I want to learn English. (*use New English 900*)
f.   I don't feel well. I think I'm getting a cold. (*stay in bed*)

3. Combine the sentences with "so."

Example: The Japanese Garden is far from here. You should take a
   bus.
   *The Japanese Garden is far from here, so you should
   take a bus.*

a.   I missed my train. I'm going to be late.
b.   The bus doesn't stop in front of my house. You'll have to walk
   a few blocks.
c.   Paulo was out of town yesterday. He couldn't attend the
   meeting.
d.   Miguel is the Morales' only son. Mrs. Morales worries about
   him.
e.   It's 9:45 now, and the last bus leaves at 10:00. We have to
   hurry.

4. Finish the sentences. Use "still."

Examples: 1. I didn't know the answer yesterday, and

   _____.
   I didn't know the answer yesterday, and I still don't.

   2. They were happily married twenty years ago, and

   _____.
   *They were happily married twenty years ago, and
   they still are.*

a.   They had bad manners when they were children, and

   _____.
b.   We were on Unit 29 two weeks ago, and _____.
c.   I couldn't find my keys all last week, and _____.
d.   He was always very thin, and _____.
e.   She was talking on the phone an hour ago, and _____.
f.   I didn't understand the lesson yesterday, and _____.

LESSON 2

520 BILL: Ali, the next bus will be here any minute.

MR. YAMAMOTO: I'm going to the Japanese Garden.

ALI: Are you Japanese? I'm from Iran.

MR. YAMAMOTO: I was born in Japan.

ALI: I went to the Japanese Garden last week.

MR. YAMAMOTO: Did you?

ALI: Yes, it's very pretty. My mother liked it very
521 much. I think it's too quiet there, but I'll go
with you if you want.521

522 MR. YAMAMOTO: Thank you. But if you come with me, your
parents won't know where you are.522

523 ALI: If you wait, I'll tell my parents where I'm
going.

524 MR. YAMAMOTO: You are a good boy. Maybe some other
time.524

525 ALI: Do you come here a lot?525 I'm here every
afternoon. My father works in that bank.
That's my friend, Mr. O'Neill, the ice
cream man.

MR. YAMAMOTO: Here's the bus. Good-bye, Ali. And thank
you.

GRAMMATICAL PREVIEW

IF-CLAUSES with the Future

If a certain condition occurs in the future, a certain action is possible. The structure of these sentences is:

IF + PRESENT TENSE, MAIN CLAUSE + FUTURE TENSE

Examples: (These four sentences mean the same thing.)

(+)	(+)
If it rains,	I'*ll* stay home.
(+)	(−)
If it rains,	I *won't* go to the park.
(−)	(+)
If it doesn't rain,	I'*ll* go to the park.
(−)	(−)
If it doesn't rain,	I *won't* stay home.

Note: The *if-clause* may also be at the end of the sentence. In that case, you leave out the comma.

Example: *I'll stay home if it rains.*

SUBSTITUTION DRILLS

1. I'll go with you if **you want.**
 I have time.
 I'm not too busy.
 it doesn't rain.

2. If you **come with me,** your parents won't know where
 you are.

 go to the Fair by yourself,
 don't call them,
 don't leave them a message,

3. **I'll tell my parents where I'm going** if you wait.
You'll miss the train
I won't be able to go with you
You won't get to the bank on time

4. What will you do if **you miss the bus?**
it rains this weekend?
you lose your job?
the car doesn't start?
you don't find your keys?

5. The next bus will be here **any minute.**
any second.
in a few minutes.
very soon.
before too long.

6. May I go with you?   —Maybe **some other time.**
some other day.
another day.
in a day or two.
next week.

7. Do you come here **a lot?**
much?
often?
very often?
regularly?

EXERCISES

1. Change both clauses to the negative.

    Example: If you wait, I'll come with you.
          If you don't wait, I won't come with you.

  a. If you find your keys, you'll be able to open the door.
  b. If I get home early, I'll bake a cake.
  c. If they leave now, they'll get to the concert on time.
  d. If it's a nice day, we'll go to the beach.
  e. If he works hard, he'll succeed in the business world.
  f. If she gets a raise, she'll be able to move to a bigger apartment.

2. Change both clauses to the affirmative.

> **Example:** If you don't call them, your parents won't know where
> you are.
> *If you call them, your parents will know where you are.*

a. If you don't write down my telephone number, you won't
    remember it later.
b. If the car doesn't start, we won't drive to work.
c. If he doesn't pass history, he won't graduate.
d. If they don't hurry, they won't get to the theater on time.
e. If she doesn't get a scholarship, she won't go to college.
f. If it's not sunny, I won't go to the park.

3. Change the first clause to the negative, and the second one to the
affirmative.

> **Example:** I'll go with you if I'm not too busy.
> *I won't go with you if I'm too busy.*

a. I'll go to the game if it doesn't snow.
b. She'll be here at six if she doesn't have to work late.
c. We'll buy a sports car if it's not too expensive.
d. You'll enjoy yourself if Mr. Crawford doesn't come to the
    party.
e. He'll lose his job if he doesn't get to work on time.
f. They'll go to the Japanese restaurant if it's not too expensive.
g. My parents will worry if I don't call them.

UNIT 31
How Marta Met Michael

LESSON 1

MIGUEL: Marta, how did you meet Michael Crawford?

526 MARTA: It's a funny story. One day while I was coming down
527 88th Street, I tripped and fell.526 My packages
528 spilled all over the sidewalk.527 I twisted my ankle,
and I couldn't stand up.528

MIGUEL: Didn't anyone help you?

529 MARTA: A couple was passing by and helped me pick up my
groceries.529 They even carried them home for me.
The guy was Michael.

MIGUEL: How long ago was that?

530 MARTA: Oh, about a year ago, I guess. Then, as we were
                  walking home, he mentioned he lived in the
531   neighborhood.₅₃₀ So I made a friend.₅₃₁ He gives
                  me English lessons, too.

    MIGUEL: But he's a painter, isn't he?

    MARTA: Yes, I think so. Why?

532 MIGUEL: I'm just putting two and two together.

    MARTA: What do you mean?

    MIGUEL: I saw a picture of Michael on Pedro's desk.*

*See Book 3, Unit 20.

GRAMMATICAL PREVIEW

1. One past action interrupts another past action.

> **Examples:** a. I *was coming* down 88th Street when I *tripped.*
> b. I *tripped* while I *was coming* down 88th Street.
> as
> when

2. One past action begins and finishes while another continues.

> **Example:** I *was sleeping* when Pedro *came* home.

3. *While* indicates *duration* and is usually followed by a verb in the past continuous form or BE in the simple past.

> **Examples:** a. I tripped *while* I *was coming* down the street.
>
> b. I typed three letters *while* you *were* out to lunch.

4. *When* indicates a completed moment of time and is usually followed by the simple past.

> **Examples:** a. I was coming down the street *when* I *tripped.*
>
> b. I was eating dinner *when* the phone *rang.*

Note: You can put the *while/as/when* clause at the beginning of the sentence.

> **Examples:** a. *While* I was coming down the street, I tripped.
> *As*
>
> b. *When* I tripped, I was coming down 88th Street.

---

*For uses of *while* and *when* with simultaneous past actions, see Book 3, Unit 24.

SUBSTITUTION DRILLS

1. While I was coming down 88th Street, I tripped and fell.
     As   running to catch the train,
                 getting on the bus,
                 walking down the stairs,
                 stepping off the curb,

2. I tripped and fell   while I was walking home.
     slipped and almost fell
     ran into Michael
     saw an accident
     dropped my bag of groceries

3. The groceries spilled all over the **sidewalk.**
                                        street.
                                        pavement.
                                        ground.
                                        floor.

4. As we were walking home,
     he **mentioned he lived in the neighborhood.**
         showed me where he used to live.
         told me about his family.
         offered to carry my suitcase.

5. He mentioned he lived nearby as we were **walking home.**
                                              crossing the street.
                                              riding on the bus.
                                              approaching my building.
                                              passing the post office.

6. So I made **a friend.**
               an enemy.
               an acquaintance.

7. I'm just **putting two and two together.**
              adding up all the facts.
              figuring something out.

CONNECTED DRILL

I **twisted my ankle,** and I couldn't **stand up.**
hurt my back,   straighten up.
broke my wrist,   move my fingers.
cut my finger,   stop the bleeding.
burned my tongue,   taste the food.

EXERCISES

1. Join the following sentences in two ways. Use *while* and *when.*

Example: I was walking down the street. I ran into Michael.
     a. *While I was walking down the street, I ran into Michael.*
     b. *I was walking down the street when I ran into Michael.*

a.   I was washing dishes. I lost my ring.
b.   Miguel hurt his back. He and Marta were trying to lift a heavy box.
c.   I was writing a letter. I heard a loud noise.
d.   Joana was making dinner. She cut her finger.
e.   Laura met Bill. She was working at the Fair.
f.   I was standing on a corner. A taxi splashed me.

2. In the sentences below, one action interrupts another. Follow the examples to fill in the verbs.

Examples: 1. I _____ (*do*) my homework when the phone _____ (*ring*).
I was doing my homework when the phone rang.

2. While I _____ (*do*) my homework, the phone _____ (*ring*).
While I was doing my homework, the phone rang.

a. Miguel _____ (*fall asleep*) while he _____ (*watch*) television.

b. While we _____ (*drive*) on the expressway, we _____ (*see*) an accident.

c. We _____ (*have*) lunch when you _____ (*call*).

d. While we _____ (*walk*) to school, it _____ (*start*) to snow.

e. I _____ (*meet*) Mr. Yamamoto while I _____ (*walk*) to the bus stop.

f. While you _____ (*play*) tennis, Michael _____ (*stop by*) to say hello.

3. Answer the questions. Use the words in parentheses.

Examples: 1. What were you doing when I called? (*eat dinner*)
I was eating dinner when you called.

2. What did you do while I was away? (*see old friends*)
I saw a lot of old friends while you were away.

a. What was Marta doing when she met Michael? (*walk home*)
b. What did Miguel do while Pedro was talking on the phone?
(*finish his homework*)
c. What were you doing when Mr. Crawford came home? (*sleep*)
d. What were you reading when I came in? (*the newspaper*)
e. What did you do while I was cooking dinner? (*clean the house*)
f. What was Laura doing when Bill last saw her? (*look for a job*)
g. Where were you going when I saw you last night? (*to the movies*)
h. What did Mr. Nikzad do while Ali was talking to Bill? (*call his wife*)
i. Who took care of your children while you were in the hospital?
(*my parents*)
j. What were you doing when it started to rain? (*play tennis*)

4. Make one sentence and add "even" for emphasis.

Example: They helped me a lot. They helped me up. They picked
up my groceries. They carried them home for me.
*They helped me up, picked up my groceries, and even
carried them home for me.*

a. I do so many things for my son and his wife. I cook their
meals. I wash their clothes. I take care of their child.
b. My brother works so much! He drives a bus during the day.
He works at a restaurant at night. He washes cars on the
weekend.
c. Laura did so many things last summer. She moved out of her
apartment. She found another job. She took a trip to Spain.
d. Ali had a great day today! He talked to Bill. He had two ice
cream sandwiches. He played ball with his father.

LESSON 2

	MARTA:	Michael and Pedro! I didn't know they knew each other.
533	MIGUEL:	Neither did I.₅₃₃ But apparently, they used to be best friends.
534	MARTA:	Really? They don't seem to have much in common.₅₃₄ What happened?
535	MIGUEL:	To make a long story short, Michael's old girlfriend fell in love with Pedro.
	MARTA:	Oh. That sounds like Pedro.
	MIGUEL:	No, it wasn't exactly Pedro's fault, but Michael wouldn't speak to him after that.
536	MARTA:	That's understandable.
	MIGUEL:	Maybe. But it's a shame.
	MARTA:	Well, Michael is sensitive. That's why he's so charming.
537	MIGUEL:	Yes, but now that Michael is seeing Joana, I hope he'll forgive Pedro.
	MARTA:	You don't have to worry about Pedro.
538	MIGUEL:	I know, but I think a good friendship deserves a second chance.
539	MARTA:	So do I, but . . .
	MIGUEL:	And Pedro needs his old friend. He's very lonely.
540	MARTA:	Lonely? Every time I see him he's with a different woman.₅₄₀

GRAMMATICAL PREVIEW

SO and NEITHER

Miguel thinks a good friendship deserves a second chance.
So does Marta.
Marta does, too.
(Marta thinks so, too.)

Marta didn't know Michael and Pedro knew each other.
Neither did Miguel.
Miguel didn't, either.

SUBSTITUTION DRILLS

1. Apparently, they used to be **best** friends.
close
good

2. They don't seem to **have much in common.**
share many interests.
be very much alike.
be like each other.

3. To make a long story short, Michael's old girlfriend fell in love
with Pedro.
In short,
In brief,
Briefly,

4. That's **understandable.**
easy to understand.
believable.
easy to believe.
reasonable.

5. Now that Michael
is seeing Joana, I hope he **will forgive Pedro.**
will call Pedro.
and Pedro will become friends again.
and Pedro will settle their differences.

6. Now that **Michael is seeing Joana, I hope he'll forgive Pedro.**
school is over, we'll be able to go on vacation.
spring is here, the weather will clear up.
the children are in college, we'll be able to go out more
often.

7. Every time I see him, he's with a different woman.
Whenever
Wherever
Every place

8. I think a good friendship deserves **a second chance.**
another try.

CONNECTED DRILLS

1. Marta **knows Michael.**   So **do** I.
    is from Colombia.   am
    went out with Pedro once.   did
    will see Miguel tonight.   will
    can speak Spanish.   can
    should talk to Joana.   should
    would like to speak English better.   would

2. Marta **lives on 87th Street.**   So **does Pedro.**
    is going to the party.   are Michael and Joana.
    was at the beach yesterday.   were Miguel and I.
    bought a new dress.   did Yolanda.

3. Bill **doesn't know Michael.**   Neither **do** I.
    isn't from Colombia.   am
    won't be home tonight.   will
    can't speak Korean.   can
    shouldn't lift heavy things.   should

EXERCISES

1. Change *too* to "so," and make all other necessary changes.

    Example: Marta knows Michael, and Pedro does, too.
             Marta knows Michael, and so does Pedro.

    a.   Michael gives free tennis lessons, and Jim does, too.
    b.   Miguel can play the guitar, and my friend can, too.
    c.   Jim should help his grandfather in the store, and his sister
        should, too.
    d.   Marta is going to the movies tonight, and Miguel is, too.
    e.   Michael used to go to an art school, and Pedro did, too.
    f.   Michael will forgive Pedro, and Marta will, too.

2. Change *either* to "neither," and make all other necessary changes.

Example: Marta didn't run into Michael this morning, and Pedro didn't, either.
Marta didn't run into Michael this morning, and neither did Pedro.

a.   Michael isn't lonely, and Joana isn't, either.
b.   Marta doesn't come from Peru, and Pedro and Miguel don't, either.
c.   The bus wasn't late this morning, and the train wasn't, either.
d.   I shouldn't leave now, and you shouldn't, either.
e.   Miguel didn't buy any groceries, and Marta didn't, either.
f.   He won't be at the party, and they won't, either.
g.   Michael can't play the piano well, and Joana can't, either.
h.   Miguel doesn't want Michael and Pedro to be enemies, and we don't, either.

3. Answer the questions with short and long answers. Use "hope."

Examples: 1. Will Michael forgive Pedro? (*yes*)
I hope so.
I hope Michael will forgive Pedro.

2. Do you have to carry that heavy bag by yourself? (*no*)
I hope not.
I hope I don't have to carry that heavy bag by myself.

a.   Can you find your way to the station? (*yes*)
b.   Did Ali disturb his father? (*no*)
c.   Did Marta hurt herself when she fell? (*no*)
d.   Is it going to clear up tomorrow? (*yes*)
e.   Will he forget to mail my letter? (*no*)
f.   Are they speaking to each other again? (*yes*)

UNIT 32
O'Neill's *Cover

LESSON 1

MR. NIKZAD:	Captain, would you tell me who is responsible for catching the thieves? I'd like to thank him personally.
CAPT. JAMISON:	You know him.
MR. NIKZAD:	I do?
541 CAPT. JAMISON:	But I must ask you not to tell anyone who he is.**541** He's one of our undercover men.
MR. NIKZAD:	Certainly.

*A *cover* is something you put on top of something else. Can you guess what it means here? How about *an undercover policeman?*

CAPT. JAMISON:		[*calling*] Sergeant O'Neill. Would you step into my office?
BILL:		Captain?
MR. NIKZAD:		Mr. O'Neill. The ice cream vendor! I don't believe it. Ali was right.
CAPT. JAMISON:		*Who* was right?
MR. NIKZAD:	**542**	My son, Ali. He never stops talking about Mr. O'Neill.**542** He always says, "Mr. O'Neill is a secret agent."
CAPT. JAMISON:		Sergeant, you didn't say anything to the boy, did you?
MR. NIKZAD:	**543** **544**	Captain, I'm sure he didn't have to. Ali is very . . . what is the word in English . . . imaginative.**543** He enjoys pretending to be you, Sergeant.**544** You are his hero.
BILL:		He's a fine boy.
MR. NIKZAD:	**545** **546**	And he loves talking to you about baseball.**545** He keeps trying to learn, but I don't know how to play, so I can't teach him.**546**

GRAMMATICAL PREVIEW
GERUNDS AND INFINITIVES

A gerund is a verb form with -ing (see*ing*, play*ing*).
An infinitive is a verb form with *to* (*to* see, *to* play).

A.

I	love like hate start continue	danc*ing*. *to* dance.

> The second verb can be in the -*ing* form or the infinitive. The meaning is the same.

B.

I	enjoy keep (on) think about gave up am tired of dislike don't mind	danc*ing*.

> The second verb can only be in the -*ing* form.

C.

I	want plan pretend intend refuse decided	*to* dance.

> The second verb can only be in the infinitive.

SUBSTITUTION DRILLS

1. I **must ask**   you not to talk about this.
   must warn
   advise
   urge
   order

2. I must ask you not to **tell the secret.**
                     leave the room.
                     come here again.
                     talk during the meeting.

3. I must ask you to **keep the secret.**
                    stay in the room.
                    stay away from here.
                    keep quiet during the meeting.

4. He never stops **talking about Mr. O'Neill.**
                     wanting to be a secret agent.
                     reading detective stories.
                     eating ice cream.
                     watching T.V.

5. He **enjoys**   pretending to be you, Sergeant.
      likes
      loves
      keeps on
      insists on

6. He loves **talking to you about baseball.**
              pretending to be an undercover agent.
              trying to solve crimes.
              following fire engines.

7. He **keeps**   trying to play baseball.
     continues
     is thinking of
     started
     stopped
     gave up

8. I don't know how to **play baseball.**
                    play the guitar.
                    ski.
                    dance.
                    speak Russian.

9. I don't know   how to play baseball.
    We are learning
    Someone is teaching her
    The teacher is showing them

10. Ali is very . . . **what is the word in English** . . . imaginative.
                  what is the English word
                  what do you say in English
                  how do you say it in English

EXERCISES

1. Change to an -*ing* form of the verb.

Example: The little girl **started to cry.**
The little girl started crying.

a.   Billy and Jack **like to ski.**
b.   Do you **prefer to listen** to records by yourself?
c.   Ali **continues to pretend** he is Mr. O'Neill.
d.   I **started to read** a detective story last night.
e.   Marta **began to study** English before she came to the United States.
f.   Ali **hates to go** to bed early.

2. Begin the sentence with the words in parentheses.

Example: Ali used to want to be a fireman. (*Last week he stopped*)
Last week he stopped wanting to be a fireman.

a.   Ali always talks about Mr. O'Neill. (*He never stops*)
b.   We ski during the winter. (*We always enjoy*)
c.   I could study Russian next semester. (*I am thinking of*)
d.   Pedro goes out with Yolanda every Friday. (*He keeps on*)
e.   Mr. Yamamoto works long hours. (*He insists on*)
f.   She's trying to lose weight. (*She should give up*)
g.   Michael and Joana were dancing all evening. (*They never stopped*)

3. Use "how to" in the sentences.

Example: I am learning to ski.
I am learning how to ski.

a.   Where did you learn to dance?
b.   Miguel is learning to drive.
c.   Mrs. Farias is teaching Joana and Paulo to cook.
d.   She is going to learn to read in school this year.
e.   No one taught me to type.

4. Answer the questions. Use "know how to."

> **Example:** Ali can't play baseball.
> Q: Why not? Won't his mother let him play?
> A: *No, it's not that. He doesn't know how to play.*

a. I can't cook dinner for you.
   Q: Why not? Don't you have time?
b. I can't type the application.
   Q: Why not? Don't you have a typewriter?
c. I can't drive you to the party.
   Q: Why not? Is there anything wrong with your car?
d. Jimmy can't read the sign.
   Q: Why not? Is there something the matter with his eyes?
e. Mary can't do the exercise.
   Q: Why not? Did she forget to bring her book home?

5. Make new sentences with "I _____ you to" or "I _____ you not to."

> **Examples:** 1. **Please don't** tell anyone who he is. It's important.
> *(must ask)*
> *I must ask you not to tell anyone who he is.*
>
> 2. You **should** be more careful. *(advise)*
> *I advise you to be more careful.*

a. You **should** tell the police about the robbery. *(advise)*
b. You **should** take the bus. It's easier than walking. *(advise)*
c. **Don't** play baseball in the street. It's dangerous. *(must warn)*
d. **Please don't** tell anyone the secret. It's important. *(must ask)*
e. **Don't** drive so fast. It's dangerous. *(must warn)*
f. You **shouldn't** be late for work. *(advise)*
g. You **really should** enter the art competition. *(urge)*
h. You **shouldn't** eat ice cream so often. You'll get sick. *(advise)*
i. **Please don't** make any noise while I'm working. It's important.
   (must ask)

LESSON 2

547 MR. NIKZAD: But tell me Sergeant, how did you know those three were thieves?

548 BILL: I suspected something right away. They kept walking back and forth in front of the bank.548

549 After watching them for three days, I knew something was going to happen soon.549

550 MR. NIKZAD: Why did you wait three days before acting?

551 BILL: We needed more proof, so I started noting their

552 movements carefully. I sold ice cream right under their noses.

553 MR. NIKZAD: I am impressed, Sergeant, impressed and grateful. But what a shame. Ali can never know he was right.

****

HUSSEIN: Ali! Did you hear? There was a robbery at Dad's bank!

ALI: Wow! Did they take a lot of money?

HUSSEIN: No. Some undercover policemen at the Fair caught the thieves.

554
555 ALI: I bet Mr. O'Neill did it! When I grow up, I want to be a secret agent like Mr. O'Neill.

HUSSEIN: Ali, Mr. O'Neill is an ice cream vendor!

SUBSTITUTION DRILLS

1. How did you know   those three were **thieves?**
          figure out   burglars?
          guess   shoplifters?
          find out   pickpockets?

2. They kept **walking back and forth in front of the bank.**
          trying to look and act like tourists.
          taking pictures of the bank entrance.
          marking things down on a yellow pad.

3. After **watching them**   for three days, I knew something was
                          going to happen soon.
      noting their behavior
      following them
      observing them

4. Why did you wait for three days before **acting?**
                        getting suspicious?
                        notifying the police?
                        arresting the suspects?

5. Did you have to wait a long time **before** phoning for help?
                         after

6. We started **noting their movements carefully.**
          watching them closely.
          following them.
          suspecting something.

7. When I grow up, I want to be a **secret agent like Mr. O'Neill.**
                         fireman like my father.
                         doctor like my mother.
                         teacher like my grandmother.

CONNECTED DRILLS

1. I am **impressed,** Sergeant, **impressed** and **grateful.**
amazed,	amazed	thankful.
surprised,	surprised	delighted.
pleased,	pleased	surprised.

2. **I sold ice cream** **right** **under their noses.**
The policeman sold ice cream	under the robbers' noses.
Hussein pinched Ali	under his father's nose.
The customer stole a watch	under the salesman's nose.
The customer stole the watch	before my eyes.

EXERCISES

1. Choose the right verb form.
   a. Ali always enjoys (*to watch/watching*) spy movies.
   b. I am tired of (*going/to go*) to school.
   c. They kept on (*to behave/behaving*) suspiciously.
   d. Don't you ever give up (*to try/trying*) to catch bank robbers?
   e. I refuse (*answering/to answer*) your questions.

2. Fill in the verb in two different forms, one with the infinitive and one with the *-ing* form.

   Example: I like _____ in restaurants. (*eat*)
               a. *I like to eat in restaurants.*
               b. *I like eating in restaurants.*

   a. We started _____ the thieves. (*follow*)
   b. When did the Sergeant begin _____ something? (*suspect*)
   c. Ali began _____ to Mr. O'Neill about baseball. (*talk*)
   d. Ali loves _____ his imagination. (*use*)
   e. Mr. Crawford likes _____ a cigar after dinner. (*have*)

3. Change the sentences. Follow the example.

   Example: Did you suspect anything before **you watched** them?
             Did you suspect anything before watching them?

   a. Bill arrested the suspects before **he called** for help.
   b. Did you hear about the accident before **you started** your trip?
   c. Ali wants to be a fireman after **he finishes** school.
   d. Did Bill remember to take his car keys before **he closed** the door?
   e. The woman walked back and forth in front of the hospital before **she went** in.
   f. We noticed the bank robbers after **we entered** the bank.
   g. Bill suspected the thieves after **he watched** them for three days.

4. Choose the right word(s) to complete the sentences.

suspect (*noun*) • **suspect** (*verb*) • **suspicious** •
suspiciously • **getting suspicious**

a.   The three men were behaving very _____.
b.   The _____ tried to look and act like a tourist.
c.   Did Bill wait three days before _____?
d.   When did Bill first _____ something was wrong?
e.   Three men slowly entered the bank at 2:20. They looked very

     _____.

UNIT 33
The Reconciliation

LESSON 1

[Michael is walking down the street. He sees Pedro. He stops.]

556	PEDRO:	It's been a long time.
557	MICHAEL:	Yes, it has.
558	PEDRO:	How have you been?
559	MICHAEL:	Much better since I spoke to you last.
	PEDRO:	You know, Michael, I'm sorry about . . .
	MICHAEL:	You don't have to be.

PEDRO: Then why are you still angry? Anyway, I *am* sorry.

MICHAEL: I am, too. I thought we were friends.

PEDRO: We were.

MICHAEL: How's Marian?

560 PEDRO: I don't know. I haven't seen her for almost three years.**560**

MICHAEL: Didn't she stay with you?

PEDRO: No. I saw her for a few weeks, and then she left. She went to Florida.

561 MICHAEL: Haven't you kept in touch?

562 PEDRO: No. There was no reason to.**562** I was happy to see her go.

MICHAEL: Then why did you . . .

PEDRO: Now wait a minute, Michael. *I* didn't go looking for *her.* She came to me.

[*Silence*]

GRAMMATICAL PREVIEW

PRESENT PERFECT TENSE with "FOR" and "SINCE"

Subject Pronouns	Auxiliary HAVE	*Past Participle	Time	
I You We They	have (+) have not (−)	lived here	since	1970. August. last Tuesday. 8:00 this morning.
He She It	has (+) has not (−)		for	eight years. two months. a few days. a short time.

Contractions

I You We They	've (+) haven't (−)
He She It	's (+) hasn't (−)

*The past participle has the same form as the past tense for regular verbs. For irregular verbs, see chart at the back of the book.

Affirmative Statement: They*'ve* lived here for a long time.

Negative Statement: They *haven't* lived here for a long time.

Negative Question: *Haven't* they lived here for a long time?

Affirmative Question: *Have* they lived here for a long time?

Answers: 1. Yes, they *have.*
2. No, they *haven't.*

Question: How long have you lived here?

Answers: 1. *Since* last August.
2. *For* nine months.

The *present perfect tense* with *for* or *since* indicates:

A. Something that began in the past and is still true now.

I have worked here since last August.
for a year.
(I got my job here last August, and I'm still working here now.)

B. The last time something happened or was true.

I haven't had a cigarette since Tuesday.
for five days.
(Today is Sunday. I had my last cigarette on Tuesday.)

SUBSTITUTION DRILLS

1. How

have	you your parents they	been?
has	Marian she Michael he	

2. **I've** been much better since I spoke to you last.
We've
They've
He's
She's
It's

3. It's been **a long time** since I saw you last.
almost a year
too long
ages

4. We've lived here since **1974.**
last August.
last summer.
June.

5. They've known each other for **a month.**
only a week.
ten years.
awhile.
some time.

6.

I We You They	**haven't**	seen Marian for almost three years.
He She	hasn't	

7. I haven't seen Marian **for the last three years.**
      in the last three years.
      since 1975.

8. I haven't spoken to Michael in **three years.**
        the last few months.
        the last couple of days.

9. You've **changed a lot**   since **I spoke to you last.**
   grown a beard   you quit your job.
   done a lot of things   you got married.
   become a vice president   last summer.
   gotten thinner   August.

10. I haven't **seen Marian**   for **a long time.**
   read a good book in   two months.
   written home   a couple of days.
   driven to work   three years.

11. I haven't **spoken to Michael** in **two weeks.**
   taken a day off   for a week.
   had a pizza   a year and a half.
   worn a suit   ages.

12. **Haven't** you kept in touch?
   Have

13. **Hasn't** Pedro kept in touch with Marian?
   Has

14. Why hasn't Pedro kept in touch? —There was no **reason to.**
              sense in it.
              call for it.
              point in doing it.

EXERCISES

1. Use "for" or "since" in the sentences below.

    a. Miguel has been living in the United States _____ a year
        now.

    b. I haven't had a cigarette _____ last September.

    c. Have you been to Joe's Bar _____ the time we went
        together?

    d. Laura hasn't spoken to Claire _____ two weeks.

    e. Hasn't Michael talked to Pedro _____ they had that big
        fight?

    f. We haven't seen you _____ a long time.

    g. They've known each other _____ they were children.

    h. They've been married _____ five years.

2. Make negative statements.

Example: He's changed since he met her.
            He hasn't changed since he met her.

    a. You've gotten thinner since I saw you last.

    b. It's been a long time since we worked together.

    c. I've worked hard in the last few weeks.

    d. They've looked very happy since they moved to the country.

    e. We've done a lot of work since we began the course.

3. Make questions.

Example: They've kept in touch with each other.
            Have they kept in touch with each other?

    a. Paulo has had a hard week at the office.

    b. You've lived in that apartment since you came to New York.

    c. He's grown a mustache since he left home.

    d. Miguel and Pedro have become good friends in the last few
        months.

    e. Laura has had some job offers this week.

    f. She's known how to swim since childhood.

    g. He's owned a car since he moved out of the city.

4. Change to the present perfect tense.

> **Example:** I was much better yesterday. (*for the last couple of days.*)
>> *I've been much better for the last couple of days.*

a. I did a lot of work last week. (*in the last few days*)
b. Gary was in Paris in May. (*for the last three weeks*)
c. She wrote five reports last month. (*in the last couple of weeks*)
d. Ali grew two inches last year. (*since last spring*)
e. We saw a lot of movies last summer. (*since they built that theater down the street*)

5. Change to the present perfect tense.

> **Example:** Paulo didn't take a day off last month. (*for a year*)
> *Paulo hasn't taken a day off for a year.*

a. Michael didn't speak to Pedro yesterday. (*for several months*)
b. We didn't drive to work last week. (*since last Monday*)
c. He didn't see Marian last year. (*for a long time*)
d. Claire and Henry weren't in the office at 11:00. (*for three hours*)
e. I didn't take the bus to work last week. (*since last Monday*)
f. She didn't do any work yesterday. (*since lunch time*)

LESSON 2

563/564   PEDRO: Michael. It's over.563 I'm sorry. What more can I
                     say?564
                     [*Silence*]
565   Let's have a beer and forget the whole thing.
                     [*Silence*]

         MICHAEL: Hello, Pedro. How have you been?
         PEDRO: Okay, Michael. It's been a long time.
566   MICHAEL: Are you still interested in photography?
567   PEDRO: Yes, and I've done a lot of new things.567 Come on,
                     I'll tell you about them.
568   MICHAEL: How's your mother? I've missed her.568
569   PEDRO: She's fine. She'll be glad to see you again. She's
570   missed you, too.569 So has the rest of my
                     family.570

GRAMMATICAL PREVIEW

More on THE PRESENT PERFECT

A. With no time indicator.

I've been to London. (During my life, I have been to London one or more times.)

B. With "lately" or "recently."

I haven't bought anything new lately.
recently.
(I haven't bought anything new in the past few weeks.)

C. With a time indicator *showing a repeated action.*

We've been to the World's Fair a number of times.
once or twice lately.
three times this week.

Tag Questions: 1. You've seen Marian lately, haven't you?
2. You haven't seen Marian lately, have you?

SUBSTITUTION DRILLS

1. Pedro has **done a lot of new things lately,** hasn't he?
        broken a lot of hearts,
        fallen in love many times,
        hurt Michael a number of times,
        gone out with a lot of women,

2. Michael hasn't **forgotten the whole thing,** has he?
        given himself a deadline,
        begun a new painting lately,
        drunk any beer recently,
        left the country,

3. You've **missed my mother,**   haven't you?
        eaten in this restaurant twice this week,
        put on some weight recently,
        swum in the Crawfords' pool,
        come here before,
        met my wife,

4. We haven't **talked for a long time,** have we?
        paid the bill,
        made a lot of progress,
        slept late all week,
        spent all the money,
        run out of money,

5. I've been away, and so **has the rest of my family.**
        have my parents.
        has she.
        have the Crawfords.

6. Michael hasn't seen Marian, and neither **has Pedro.**
        have Bill and I.
        has Marta.
        have we.

7. It's over.
    ended.
    finished.
    forgotten.
    done with.
    in the past.

8. What more can I say?
        else

9. Let's have a beer and forget the whole thing.
                      start all over again.
                      be friends.
                      talk over old times.
                      catch up on everything.

10. Are you still interested in photography?
                              philosophy?
                              archaeology?
                              psychology?
                              astrology?
                              astronomy?
                              chemistry?
                              linguistics?
                              law?
                              medicine?
                              art?
                              music?
                              literature?

CONNECTED DRILLS

1. I've **missed your mother.** —**She's missed you,** too.
     had enough to drink.   —I have,
     helped Laura before.   —She's helped you,
     given up on Pedro.   —Marta has,

2. I haven't **had a beer for a long time.** —**Michael hasn't,** either.
     been to the beach lately.   —She hasn't,
     read the paper all week.   —They haven't,
     seen any new movies recently. —The Farias's haven't,

EXERCISES

1. Make tag questions.

> **Examples:** 1. Pedro has done a lot of things.
> *Pedro has done a lot of things, hasn't he?*
>
> 2. We haven't seen each other for a long time.
> *We haven't seen each other for a long time, have we?*

    a. Ali hasn't drunk all his milk.
    b. I've given you my address.
    c. They've begun a new project.
    d. Ali's had ice cream twice this week.
    e. You haven't forgotten anything.
    f. You and I haven't gone to a party in ages.
    g. It has gotten cloudy.

2. Respond to the statements.

> **Examples:** 1. I've missed your mother. (*She*)
> *She's missed you, too.*
>
> 2. Marian hasn't kept in touch with you. (*I*)
> *I haven't kept in touch with her, either.*

    a. Pedro has forgotten Marian. (*His mother*)
    b. I haven't been to the Fair all week. (*Laura*)
    c. They've had enough to eat. (*I*)
    d. Paulo has taken the week off. (*Henry*)
    e. You haven't called Claire lately. (*She*)
    f. Michael hasn't seen Gary recently. (*The Crawfords*)

3. Use the present perfect in each sentence.

a. Pedro _____ Miguel since he was fifteen. (*know*)
b. You _____ a lot of progress in this course. (*make*)
c. You _____ that dress before, haven't you? (*wear*)
d. I _____ three glasses of water. I'm still thirsty. (*drink*)
e. You don't think Miguel _____ in love with Marta, do you? (*fall*)
f. _____ you _____ any new clothes lately? (*get*)
g. Peggy _____ at least six inches since the last time we saw her. (*grow*)

4. Use "since" or "for" in the sentences.

Examples: 1. The Ortegas don't live in Colombia now. They left there ten years ago.
The Ortegas haven't lived in Colombia for ten years.

2. Pedro doesn't study English now. He stopped studying it when he graduated from high school.
Pedro hasn't studied English since he graduated from high school.

a. Laura doesn't work for Mr. Crawford now. She quit her job at the beginning of the summer.
b. Michael and Pedro don't talk to each other now. They had a big fight three years ago.
c. Marian doesn't write to Pedro now. She stopped writing to him when she moved to Florida.
d. I don't drive to the office now. I sold my car six months ago.
e. Mr. Nikzad doesn't eat at the cafeteria now. He stopped eating there when he found a hair in his soup.
f. Pedro doesn't go out with Yolanda now. She got engaged to someone else a month ago.
g. Ali didn't have an ice cream sandwich today or yesterday. The last time he had one was the day before yesterday.

UNIT 34
Reading and Refocus

LESSON 1

Michael's Block

571   Eighty-eighth Street is usually a busy street, especially
572 during the summer.₅₇₁ But sometimes, early in the morning
and in the heat of the afternoon, it is quiet.₅₇₂ No, not
573 "quiet", quiet*er*. There are always kids playing ball. They
don't seem to notice the heat, the darkness, or the passing
cars.₅₇₃

574   It's a street like many others.574 Children run, and jump,
575   and fall. Parents push baby carriages. Young men and women
walk slowly, arm in arm, or hand in hand.575 The people of
576   the neighborhood know each other. When friends meet, they
stop and say a word or two.576
577   Two women, both lost in thought, walk toward each
578   other.577 As they pass, they look up.578 They stop. They smile.
They start to speak at the same time. They laugh, happy to
579   see each other. After a minute or two, one turns around and
walks the other to her door.579 They stand and talk a few
580   minutes more. Then each one takes a few steps, turns, and
waves good-bye.580

Questions about "Michael's Block"

Fact:
The answers are *clear* in the story.

1. What is 88th Street like?
2. Is it ever quieter than usual?
3. Is 88th Street busier in the summer or in the winter?
4. Which character in this book lives on 88th Street?
5. Are the two women thinking about something as they walk toward each other?
6. Were the two women walking in the same or opposite directions when they met?

Inference:
You can *guess the right answers* from the story.

1. Are there usually a lot of people on 88th Street, or is it usually empty?
2. Why is the street never completely quiet?
3. Is 88th Street a friendly or an unfriendly place?
4. What sport do the kids on the block enjoy?
5. Did the two women have a lot to say to each other?
6. Does one of the two women live on 88th Street?

To the Student:
There are *no wrong answers* to these questions.

1. Do you live in a big city, in a small town, or in the country?
2. Is your street noisy or quiet?
3. Are there many young children on your street?
4. Is your neighborhood different in the winter than it is in the summer?
5. What do you like most about your neighborhood?
6. Are you usually lost in thought when you walk down the street, or do you notice people and things around you?

USING YOUR ENGLISH

ARTICLES: A, THE, and Ø (no article)

A. As with many other grammatical rules, the use of the article depends on what the speaker is thinking.

1. The INDEFINITE ARTICLE "A" or "AN" indicates a GENERAL and SINGULAR noun:
   I need a pen. (any pen)

2. No ARTICLE (Ø) indicates a GENERAL and PLURAL noun:
   I like movies. (all movies)
   I like literature. (all literature)
   I like ice cream. (all ice cream)

3. The DEFINITE ARTICLE "THE" indicates:

   a. a SPECIFIC and SINGULAR noun:
      I like the (English) textbook.

   b. SPECIFIC and PLURAL nouns:
      I like the plays (of Shakespeare).

   c. SPECIFIC and NON-COUNT nouns:
      I like the literature (of the 20th century).
      I like the ice cream (at the Fair).

B. Look at the italicized nouns in the following sentences. What do you think the speaker means? Are the nouns *specific* or *general?* Are they *singular, plural,* or *non-count?*

Follow the examples in 1, 2, and 3.

1. The passing *car*ᵃ splashed *water*ᵇ on the *people.* ᶜ
   a. *specific, singular*
   b. *general, non-count*
   c. *specific, plural*

2. They don't seem to notice the *heat* on 88th Street.
   specific, non-count

3. *Heat*ᵃ doesn't bother him; he comes from a warm *country.* ᵇ
   a. *general, non-count*
   b. *general, singular*

4. I live in a large *building* on 36th Street.

5. I live in the large *building* on 36th Street.

6. Small *boys*ᵃ don't notice *darkness*ᵇ when they're playing.

7. The two *lovers*ᵃ didn't mind the *darkness.* ᵇ

8. Passing *cars*ᵃ frequently splash *water*ᵇ on *people*ᶜ when it's raining hard.

9. True *love* is beautiful.

10. I'll see you before *dinner.*

11. I'll see you before the *dinner*ᵃ for the *President.* ᵇ

12. Japanese *history* is interesting.

13. The *history* of Japan is interesting.

14. *Flowers* are beautiful.

15. The *flowers* in my garden are still alive.

C. Special Uses

1. Many common nouns don't use articles when they appear in the following general expressions:

a.	GO TRAVEL LEAVE *by* COME	bus car train plane	b. BE *in* c. GO *to*	bed school college church prison

Examples: a. *He went to bed early last night.*
b. *We always travel by plane.*
c. *He's in prison. He robbed a bank.*

2. The names of countries *usually don't* need "THE."
              continents
              cities
              streets
              holidays

Here are some common exceptions:

the Champs Elysees	the Netherlands	the United Arab Republic
the Dominican Republic	the Philippines	the United Kingdom
the Gambia	the Soviet Union	the United States
the Hague	the Sudan	the West Indies

3. Normally, the names of geographical features require the article.

Examples: the Atlantic Ocean
                  the Sahara Desert
                  the Amazon River

D. Now, use A, AN, THE, or Ø (no article) in the sentences below.

1. There are three countries in _____ North America:
   _____ Canada, _____ United States, and
   _____ Mexico.

2. Juan was born in _____ Cuba, but his parents moved to
   _____ Dominican Republic when he was a child.

3. Many children like _____ Christmas better than
   _____ Independence Day because they get presents on
   _____ Christmas.

4. Nora likes to go downtown and shop on _____
   Fourteenth Street because _____ stores are interesting
   and inexpensive.

5. Bill got home late and wanted to go right to _____ bed.

6. _____ Panama Canal is between _____ Atlantic
   Ocean and _____ Pacific.

7. After Bill caught the robbers, they went to _____ prison.

8. I went to _____ church last Sunday.

9. I went to _____ church on 88th Street, not my usual one.

10. I like to work at _____ night.

E. Use A, AN, THE, or Ø in the paragraphs below. Sometimes there is one correct answer. Sometimes your answer depends on what you want to say.

KENNEDY SQUARE

_____ square is usually _____ noisy place, especially during _____ summer. But sometimes, early in _____ morning and in _____ cool of _____ evening, it is peaceful. There are usually _____ kids playing ball, but darkness and their mothers make them go home by 8:00.

But not every child is home by 8:00. Some stay out to watch _____ world at _____ night. They watch _____ streets grow dark, and _____ lights go on. They stand and watch _____ adults in the neighborhood come out for _____ evening.

LESSON 2

Sergeant O'Neill's Report

At noon on June 3, three men bought sandwiches and ice cream and sat on one of the benches in front of the International Bank. This behavior continued on June 4 and 5.

581 They were trying to look and act like tourists, but they obviously were not.581 They never smiled. They were not enjoying themselves. The suspects carefully noted the

582 movements of each of the bank's employees. They even noted when and where I moved my ice cream cart.582

583 On June 5, at exactly 2:20, when two of the four guards were out to lunch, the three suspects moved toward the

584 entrance of the bank.583 I immediately called for help.584 Then I moved the ice cream cart closer to the entrance of

585 the bank. I wanted to be able to stop them from leaving the area.585

One of the suspects stood at the door of the bank. The other two entered the bank and stood in line. When they got

586 up to the tellers, they took guns out of paper bags. Most of the people in the bank didn't know what was happening.586 I could see this through the windows of the bank.

587 Meanwhile, the other non-uniformed policemen arrived.587

588 We *spread out. Some went into the bank and some stood near the front.588 We wanted to wait until they had the

589 money in their hands. Then we got them.589 It was all over in twenty seconds.

590 I never stopped selling ice cream, although I gave one man too much change.

---

*spread out means "divided into smaller groups and went in different directions."

WORLD'S FAIR POLICE DEPARTMENT

COMPLAINT REPORT

Mr. H. A. Nikzad
COMPLAINANT'S NAME

Bank Robbery
NATURE OF COMPLAINT

SERIAL NUMBER

145-58 4th Ave.
COMPLAINANT'S ADDRESS

PHONE NUMBER

World's Fair Bank, Plaza of the Nations
LOCATION OF OFFENSE OR INCIDENT

Sgt. William O'Neil
REPORTED BY

ADDRESS

PHONE NUMBER

Capt. Jamison
RECEIVED BY

1:24
TIME

June 3, 1976
DATE

OFFICERS ASSIGNED

HOW REPORTED

DETAILS OF COMPLAINT, OR INCIDENT

PERSONS ARRESTED_____NO._3_____   _____NO_____

CASE CLOSED:_____UNFOUNDED:_____CLEARED BY ARREST:_____OTHER_____

APPROVED_____SIGNED_____DATE_____

OFFENSE REPORT

DESCRIPTION OF PROPERTY

	ESTIMATED VALUE	RECOVERED	
		DATE	VALUE
TOTAL			

I HEREBY ACKNOWLEDGE RECEIPT OF THE ABOVE RECOVERED ARTICLES DELIVERED TO ME

BY_____   SIGNED_____   DATE_____

DESCRIPTION OF SUSPECTS OR PERSONS WANTED:

Questions about "Sergeant Weizman's Report"

Fact:
The answers are *clear* in the story.

1. Where did the suspects sit after they bought sandwiches and ice cream?
2. Did they behave the same or differently on June 4 and 5?
3. Were all of the guards out to lunch at 2:20 on June 5?
4. Where was Bill while the robbery was going on?
5. Did all or some of the police go into the bank?
6. Did the arrest take a long time?

Inference:
You can *guess the right answers* from the story.

1. Did Bill get suspicious the first time he saw the three men or only after watching them for awhile?
2. Why didn't the suspects seem like tourists?
3. Did the suspects know what time the guards went out to lunch?
4. Did all of the suspects go into the bank at 2:20?
5. Why didn't Bill arrest them before they entered the bank?
6. Did Bill's customers know what was happening or not?

To the Student:
There are *no wrong answers* to these questions.

1. Why didn't the suspects notice the police?
2. How does a tourist act? How do you act on vacation?
3. Do you think Bill and his men handled the attempted robbery well?
4. Do you think Bill's report is clear, or does it need more information?
5. Are there ever any bank robberies in your country?
6. Do you think movies about bank robberies give people criminal ideas or not?

USING YOUR ENGLISH

I. ALTHOUGH

A. We use *although* to join two seemingly contradictory ideas or expectations.

Example: *Although I broke my leg, I am going to go to work tomorrow.*

(We do not expect a person with a broken leg to go to work the next day.)

The *although* clause can sometimes come after the main clause, too. (See Sentence 590)

B. Join the following sentences. Use *although.*

Example: I broke my leg.
I'm going to work tomorrow.
Although I broke my leg, I'm going to go to work tomorrow.

1. It was raining.
   I took a walk through the garden.
2. I am getting fat.
   I still eat two desserts with each meal.
3. I have a lot of money.
   I am afraid to spend it.
4. I ate chicken last night.
   I want it again tonight.
5. We are working ten hours a day.
   We are still behind.
6. The Mayor is very unpopular.
   He thinks he can win the election.
7. We aren't rich.
   We are happy.
8. English is difficult.
   I know I can learn it.

II. BE ABLE TO

A. *Be able to* means the same as "can." We usually prefer to use "can."

Example: *I can read and write English.* (preferred)
I am able to read and write English.

After a verb or a modal we *must* use BE ABLE TO.

Example: *I wanted to be able to stop them.*

B. Use BE ABLE TO in the sentences below.

1. By the year 2050 we should _____ travel to the moon for a vacation.

2. He would like to _____ study in Paris. Unfortunately, his parents are poor.

3. They must _____ buy everything they want. They are very rich.

4. He wants to _____ live comfortably in his old age.

5. She has to _____ study in peace. If she can't, she won't pass her exams.

6. I'm too busy to take a vacation now. I'll _____ take one two months from now.

7. You have many skills. You should _____ get that job.

III. Joining ideas with AND and OR

A. Look for the word or idea that is different. Then join the
   following pairs of sentences. Follow the examples.

Examples: 1. They noted **when** I moved my cart.
   They noted **where** I moved my cart.
   They noted when and where I moved my cart.

2. They didn't notice **when** I moved my cart.
   They didn't notice **where** I moved my cart.
   *They didn't notice when or where I moved my
   cart.*

B. 1. I have often wondered where my parents met.
   I have often wondered how my parents met.
2. Do they know how rich he is?
   Do they know how famous he is?
3. They were trying to look like tourists.
   They were trying to act like tourists.
4. I can't remember where I met her.
   I can't remember when I met her.
5. They have well-educated children.
   They have polite children.
6. She lives in New York.
   She works in New York.
7. They don't look like teenagers.
   They don't act like teenagers.
8. We like to sing all night.
   We like to dance all night.
9. Nobody knows who he is.
   Nobody knows what he does for a living.
10. The robbers didn't try to fight.
    The robbers didn't try to run away.

LESSON 3

Joe's

Michael and Pedro are sitting in a corner of "Joe's". Listen to the bartender...

591
592   "I like this old bar. I know it's old-fashioned, but that's what I like about it.**591** Sure, it's dark. Most bars are. But that's all right, some things look better in the dark.**592**
593
594   Besides, you don't go to a bar to read, do you?**593** This is a friendly place. You can get a beer on your way home from work, find some friends, relax, and forget about your kids,
595   your job, and your mother-in-law.**594** Times are changing, but
596   'Joe's' stays the same.**595** Oh, there's a difference. This kind
597   of place used to be 'for men only.'**596** Now, everybody's
598   welcome.**597** If your money's good, we're glad to have you.**598**
599   I've been a bartender here for thirty years, and I'm still
600   happy to come to work and see the old mahogany bar.**599** It still makes me happy to see the liquor bottles beside the old French mirror.**600** It's not a bad life. And, you know, it's funny. I don't drink."

Questions about "Joe's"

Fact:
The answers are *clear* in the story.

1. Is "Joe's" modern or old-fashioned?
2. Does the bartender like it?
3. What are some things people do at this bar?
4. Is this bar still "for men only," or can women go there, too?
5. How long has this man been a bartender?
6. Isn't he tired of being a bartender?

Inference:
You can *guess the right answers* from the story.

1. Is "Joe's" a fancy place?
2. What does the bartender mean when he says, "Some things look better in the dark"?
3. Why can't you read easily in a bar like this one?
4. Does this bar do a good business?
5. Does the bartender like how modern times have changed this bar or not?
6. Does the bartender like to talk, or is he a quiet, shy person?

To the Student:
There are *no wrong answers* to these questions.

1. Which do you prefer, old-fashioned or modern places?
2. Where do you go outside your home to relax and forget your troubles?
3. Have you ever worked in a restaurant?
4. Do you have a favorite restaurant in your city?
5. Have you noticed any big changes in your city in the last few years, or are things the same as they've always been?
6. Why do you think "Joe's" changed its rule about women?

USING YOUR ENGLISH

I. The HYPHEN (-)

A. We use the hyphen to join words or parts of words. The hyphen has many uses, but here, we will look at only a few. We have seen the hyphen in: 1. numbers (*twenty-one* to *ninety-nine*) and 2. phrases (*a one-day vacation*).

In this unit we will look at hyphenated adjectives such as *old-fashioned* (see Sentence 591). These adjectives have two parts. The first part is an adjective or noun form. The last part is a verb form.

Examples: 1 *chocolate-covered*   (covered with chocolate)
2. *American-built*   (built by Americans)
3. *man-made*   (made by men)
4. *self-taught*   (taught by the person himself)

Hyphenated adjectives are usually adjectives of *condition.*

B. Make hyphenated adjectives from these phrases. Follow the examples above.

1. made by machine
2. covered with ice cream
3. filled with fruit
4. painted by hand
5. lined with trees
6. washed by machine

II. Adjective Order

A. As you know, English speakers use adjectives in a certain order. We have studied adjectives of *opinion, size, condition, age,* and *color.* (For review see Book 2, Units 13, 18, 21; and Book 3, Unit 27)

In this unit we will look at the order of adjectives of *nationality* and *material*. (For a list of adjectives of nationality see Unit 7.) Remember to capitalize adjectives of nationality.

CHART 1: Order of Adjectives of *Nationality* and *Material*

Age	Nationality	Material	Noun
old		mahogany	bar
old	French		mirror
new	Italian	marble	table

CHART 2: Here are some more examples. We rarely use more than three adjectives before a noun.

Condition	Size	Age	Nationality	Material	Noun
		modern	French	silver	coin
beautiful	large		foreign		car
		antique	American	glass	bottle

B. Look at the sentences below. Now rewrite them to include the adjectives following the sentences. Put the adjectives in correct order.

1. Give me the book on the _____ _____ table. (*mahogany, African*) ,

2. _____ _____ coffee is delicious. (*Italian, strong*)

3. _____ _____ _____ jewelry is beautiful. (*gold, ancient, Egyptian*)

4. For my birthday, my parents bought me a _____ _____ _____ blouse. (*Chinese, old, silk*)

5. When he retired, they gave him a _____ _____ _____ watch. (*Swiss-made, gold, new*)

III. THE FAMILY TREE

A. Study the chart below. On it you will find all the common family relationships in English speaking countries.

B. Use the right word. Who's who?

1. Your husband's or wife's mother is your _____.
2. Your father's or mother's sister is your _____.
3. Your aunt's or uncle's child is your _____.
4. Your son's wife is your _____.
5. Your sister's or brother's female child is your _____.
6. Your husband's or wife's brother is your _____.
7. Your father's or mother's brother is your _____.
8. Your daughter's husband is your _____.
9. Your sister's or brother's male child is your _____.
10. Your child's son is your _____.
11. Your child's daughter is your _____.

THE FAMILY TREE

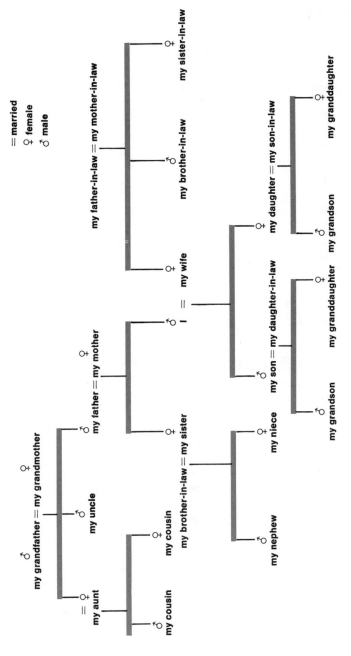

= married
♀ female
♂ male

my grandfather = my grandmother

my uncle

my aunt

my cousin

my cousin

my cousin

my father = my mother

I = my wife

my brother-in-law = my sister

my father-in-law = my mother-in-law

my brother-in-law

my sister-in-law

my son = my daughter-in-law

my daughter = my son-in-law

my niece

my nephew

my grandson

my granddaughter

my grandson

my granddaughter

IRREGULAR VERBS

I. ALL THREE FORMS ARE THE SAME

BASE, PAST, PAST PARTICIPLE

bet
cost
cut
hit
hurt
knit
let
put
quit
rid
set
shut
split
spread

II. TWO FORMS ARE THE SAME

BASE	PAST + PAST PARTICIPLE
bend	bent
build	built
lend	lent
send	sent
spend	spent
bleed	bled
feed	fed
hold	held
lead	led
read	*read
feel	felt
keep	kept
leave	left

*Pronounced "red."

BASE	PAST + PAST PARTICIPLE
mean	meant
meet	met
sleep	slept
hang	hung
stick	stuck
win	won
bring	brought
buy	bought
fight	fought
think	thought
catch	caught
teach	taught
find	found
take	took
lose	lost
shine	shone
shoot	shot
sell	sold
tell	told
become	became
come	came
run	ran
have	had
hear	heard
make	made
pay	paid
say	said
sit	sat
stand	stood

III. ALL THREE FORMS ARE DIFFERENT

BASE	PAST	PAST PARTICIPLE
break	broke	broken
choose	chose	chosen
freeze	froze	frozen
speak	spoke	spoken
steal	stole	stolen
wake	woke	waked
tear	tore	torn
wear	wore	worn
grow	grew	grown
know	knew	known
throw	threw	thrown
bite	bit	bitten
hide	hid	hidden
take	took	taken
drive	drove	driven
ride	rode	ridden
write	wrote	written
begin	began	begun
drink	drank	drunk
ring	rang	rung
sing	sang	sung
swim	swam	swum
eat	ate	eaten
fall	fell	fallen
do	did	done
draw	drew	drawn
fly	flew	flown
get	got	gotten
forget	forgot	forgotten
give	gave	given
go	went	gone
lie	lay	lain
see	saw	seen

NEW ENGLISH 900

THE INTONATION LINES

The next ten pages contain the 150 Base Sentences found in this book. They are arranged by unit. The sentences are not accompanied by the context in which they appear in the actual lessons.

The blue lines that appear with a sentence indicate how it is spoken in American English. If you look at the lines you will be able to recognize the basic intonation patterns of English. The language employs three pitches: low, medium, and high.

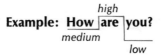

The intonation lines should not be used independently, but should be studied along with the sentences as they are spoken, either by your teacher or on the tapes that accompany the book. It is not really possible to learn how to produce a sound by studying only a printed representation of that sound. As you repeat the sentences aloud after your teacher or after the tapes, you will gradually become familiar with the intonation patterns and learn how to use them.

451 Let's sit down for a few minutes. **452** I can clean up later.

453 I can do it by myself in the morning.

454 It's too bad Paulo had to work late. **455** I could tell.

456 As a matter of fact, you made everybody feel comfortable.

457 I was tired of giving parties by myself.

458 You know, when I was a teenager, I used to go to parties all the time.

459 I enjoyed myself every minute—parties, dances, boys.

460 I used to live from dance to dance.

461 On the weekends, Paulo and I never used to be home.

462 It's a long story. **463** Then I'll tell you about myself.

464 This kitchen is too small for two. **465** Make yourself at home.

466 How did they like it? **467** Very much.

468 In fact, we're starting the project immediately.

469 And guess who's in charge? **470** You give up too easily.

471 You work harder than anyone else in that office.

472 You even eat more quickly than you used to.

473 He paints better than anyone I know.

474 We won't announce the contest until Mr. Crawford finishes the brochure.

475 It's large enough, and modern and businesslike.

476 And very formal—too formal, perhaps.

477 Either he does well this year, or he gives up art and goes into business with his father.

478 How well is "well"? **479** How is he going to measure success?

480 Does he have to paint as well as the masters?

481 He looks just like me, you know, Joana.

482 At least he used to.

483 He's eighteen months older than I am, but as kids we used to wear the same clothes and pretend we were twins!

484 He was too busy.

485 Gary and I went to the same college, but that's when things started to change.

486 Because my father wanted him to.

487 Gary and I saw each other less and less.

488 When Gary graduated, he went to work for my father.

489 Like my father, Gary was always busy.

490 He never forgets a face.

491 I would like to write about two people, a man and a woman.

492 They live quiet lives.

493 When they go out into the street, no one asks for their autographs, but everyone in their profession knows and respects them.

494 They work as a team.

495 They met on their first job.

496 The magazine sent them all over the world to cover important events.

497 One day the magazine went bankrupt.

498 Many other magazines and newspapers offered them positions, but at this point the man and the woman decided to work independently.

499 He wanted to work on a photographic essay of bonsai.

500 For once, they did not worry about deadlines and editors.

501 Don't feel so sorry for yourself.

502 Nobody likes to get out and look for a job.

503 I'm getting depressed again.

504 It's time for a change.

505 I don't hate work — that's why I got the job with Crawford — but I don't like offices.

506 I'd rather work with people than with files and typewriters.

507 I could be a real estate agent, a travel agent, a . . . anything, as long as it isn't boring.

508 I think I'd like to be my own boss.

509 I must be getting hungry.

510 Maybe I'm getting a cold.

511 Can you tell me where the Japanese Garden is?

512 It's quite a long walk from here.

513 It stops right over there, in the Plaza of Nations.

514 Between the statue and the fountain.

515 Would you do me a favor?

516 Would you take this gentleman to the bus stop over there?

517 My father says I shouldn't ask so many questions.

518 So I'm sorry.   **519** But I still want to know.

520 Ali, the next bus will be here any minute.

521 I think it's too quiet there, but I'll go with you if you want.

522 But if you come with me, your parents won't know where you are.

523 If you wait, I'll tell my parents where I'm going.

524 Maybe some other time.

525 Do you come here a lot?

526 One day while I was coming down 88th Street, I tripped and fell.

527 My packages spilled all over the sidewalk.

528 I twisted my ankle, and I couldn't stand up.

529 A couple was passing by and helped me pick up my groceries.

530 Then, as we were walking home, he mentioned he lived in the neighborhood.

531   So I made a friend.

532   I'm just putting two and two together.

533   Neither did I.

534   They don't seem to have much in common.

535   To make a long story short, Michael's old girlfriend fell in love with Pedro.

536   That's understandable.

537   Yes, but now that Michael is seeing Joana, I hope he'll forgive Pedro.

538   I know, but I think a good friendship deserves a second chance.

539   So do I, but . . .

540   Every time I see him he's with a different woman.

541   But I must ask you not to tell anyone who he is.

542   He never stops talking about Mr. O'Neill.

543   Ali is very . . . what is the word in English . . . imaginative.

544   He enjoys pretending to be you, Sergeant.

545 And he loves talking to you about baseball.

546 He keeps trying to learn, but I don't know how to play, so I can't teach him.

547 But tell me Sergeant, how did you know those three were thieves?

548 They kept walking back and forth in front of the bank.

549 After watching them for three days, I knew something was going to happen soon.

550 Why did you wait three days before acting?

551 We needed more proof, so I started noting their movements carefully.

552 I sold ice cream right under their noses.

553 I am impressed, Sergeant, impressed and grateful.

554 I bet Mr. O'Neill did it!

555 When I grow up, I want to be a secret agent like Mr. O'Neill.

556 It's been a long time.   **557** Yes, it has.

558 How have you been?

559 Much better since I spoke to you last.

560 I haven't seen her for almost three years.

561 Haven't you kept in touch?

562 There was no reason to.   **563** It's over.

564 What more can I say?

565 Let's have a beer and forget the whole thing.

566 Are you still interested in photography?

567 Yes, and I've done a lot of new things.

568 I've missed her.

569 She's missed you, too.

570 So has the rest of my family.

571 Eighty-eighth Street is usually a busy street, especially during the summer.

572 But sometimes, early in the morning and in the heat of the afternoon, it is quiet.

573 They don't seem to notice the heat, the darkness, or the passing cars.

574 It's a street like many others.

575 Young men and women walk slowly, arm in arm, or hand in hand.

576 When friends meet, they stop and say a word or two.

577 Two women, both lost in thought, walk toward each other.

578 As they pass, they look up.

579 After a minute or two, one turns around and walks the other to her door.

580 Then each one takes a few steps, turns, and waves good-bye.

581 They were trying to look and act like tourists, but they obviously were not.

582 They even noted when and where I moved my ice cream cart.

583 On June 5, at exactly 2:20, when two of the four guards were out to lunch, the three suspects moved toward the entrance of the bank.

584 I immediately called for help.

585 I wanted to be able to stop them from leaving the area.

586 Most of the people in the bank didn't know what was happening.

587 Meanwhile, the other non-uniformed policemen arrived.

588 Some went into the bank and some stood near the front.

589 Then we got them.

590 I never stopped selling ice cream although I gave one man too much change.

591 I know it's old-fashioned, but that's what I like about it.

592 But that's all right, some things look better in the dark.

593 Besides, you don't go to a bar to read, do you?

594 You can get a beer on your way home from work, find some friends, relax, and forget about your kids, your job, and your mother-in-law.

595 Times are changing, but 'Joe's' stays the same.

596 This kind of place used to be 'for men only.'

597 Now, everybody's welcome.

598 If your money's good, we're glad to have you.

599 I've been a bartender here for thirty years, and I'm still happy to come to work and see the old mahogany bar.

600 It still makes me happy to see the liquor bottles beside the old French mirror.

NEW ENGLISH 900

WORD INDEX

On the following pages you will find a list of the words that appear in this book. They are arranged in alphabetical order. Each word is followed by a sentence.

like I don't like dinner parties.

This is the sentence in which the word first appears in context in the book. Following the sentence, two numbers are given.

our Are those students in our class? 3/1

These numbers indicate the unit and lesson in which the word and sentence appear. That is, 5/2 means Unit Five, Lesson Two.

Nouns are listed under the singular form, even if in the book they appeared in the plural.

friend Where are my friends?

Verbs are listed under the base form.

wait I'm sorry to keep you waiting.

The only exceptions to the above are irregular forms.

was I was in the bathroom.

Phrases, idioms, and other units of meaning that consist of more than one word are listed separately.

good morning Good morning, sir.

This index is not intended to be a substitute for a dictionary, but you will often be able to understand a word from the sentence given with it. You can also refer back to the particular unit and lesson to study the word in a larger context.

accident	I saw an accident while I was walking home. 31/1
add	I'm just adding up all the facts. 31/1
advise	I advise you not to talk about this. 32/1
afraid	I am afraid of living alone. 27/1
ages	I haven't worn a suit for ages. 33/1
alike	They don't seem to be very much alike. 31/2
although	I never stopped selling ice cream, although I gave one man too much change. 34/2
amazed	I am amazed, Sergeant, amazed and thankful. 32/2
ankle	I twisted my ankle, and I co n't stand up. 31/1
apparent	But, apparently, they used to be best friends. 31/2
approach	He mentioned that he lived nearby as we were approaching my building. 31/1
area	We won't announce the contest until we find the right exhibition area. 28/2
arrest	Why did you wait for three days before arresting the suspects? 32/2
asleep	It's too bad Paulo fell asleep during the movie. 27/1
autograph	When they go out into the street, no one asks for their autographs, but everyone in their profession knows and respects them. 29/2
award	They won many awards and medals. 29/2
bag	I dropped my bag of groceries while I was walking home. 31/1
ball	There are always kids playing ball. 34/1
bankrupt	One day the magazine went bankrupt. 29/2
bar	I like this old bar. 34/3
bartender	I've been a bartender here for thirty years, and I'm still happy to come to work and see the old mahogany bar. 34/3
battle	When there are battles in the Middle East, they are there. 29/2
become	Now that Michael is seeing Joana, I hope he and Pedro will become friends again. 31/2
been	It's been a long time. 33/1
begun	Michael hasn't begun a new painting lately, has he? 33/2
bench	At noon on June 3, three men bought sandwiches and ice cream, and sat on one of the benches in front of the International Bank. 34/2
beside	It still makes me happy to see the liquor bottles beside the old French mirror. 34/3
besides	Besides, you don't go to a bar to read, do you? 34/3
bet	I bet Mr. O'Neill did it! 32/2
bleed	I cut my finger, and I couldn't stop the bleeding. 31/1
boutique	Joana worked in a boutique until she came to New York. 28/2
burglar	How did you figure out those three were burglars? 32/2
burn	I burned my tongue, and I couldn't taste the food. 31/1

carriage	Parents push baby carriages. 34/1
carry	As we were walking home, he offered to carry my suitcase. 31/1
cart	They even noted when and where I moved my ice cream cart. 34/2
casual	His office is too casual. 28/2
catch	As I was running to catch the train, I tripped and fell. 31/1
caught	Some undercover policemen at the Fair caught the thieves. 32/2
chance	Then this competition could be his big chance. 28/2
charge	And guess who's in charge? 28/1
choose	We won't announce the contest until my boss chooses the judges. 28/2
clean	Michael cleans less carefully than anyone I know. 28/1
close	We started watching them closely. 32/2
comfortable	As a matter of fact, you made everybody feel comfortable. 27/1
common	They don't seem to have much in common. 31/2
conservative	Is Paulo a conservative dresser? 28/1
contact	How did Paulo contact Mr. Crawford? 28/2
contest	We won't announce the contest until Mr. Crawford finishes the brochure. 28/2
cost	We won't announce the contest until we know the cost. 28/2
cross	Could you help this woman cross the street? 30/1
cup	How about a cup of coffee? 27/2
curb	As I was stepping off the curb, I tripped and fell. 31/1
cut	I cut myself. 27/2
darkness	They don't seem to notice the heat, the darkness, or the passing cars. 34/1
deadline	For once, they did not worry about deadlines and editors. 29/2
delighted	I am surprised, Sergeant, surprised and delighted. 32/2
deserve	I know, but I think a good friendship deserves a second chance. 31/2
detective	He never stops reading detective stories. 32/1
diaper	I couldn't change diapers when I was single, but I can now. 27/1
difference	Now that Michael is seeing Joana, I hope he and Pedro will settle their differences. 31/2
directly	The Fair bus stops right over there, directly opposite the Japanese Garden. 30/1
done	You've done a lot of things since you got married. 33/1
driven	I haven't driven to work in three years. 33/1
drunk	Michael hasn't drunk any beer recently, has he? 33/2
dust	I can dust later. 27/1

earthquake	When there are earthquakes in Honduras, they are there. 29/2
eaten	You've eaten in this restaurant twice this week, haven't you? 33/2
efficient	Does he work efficiently? 28/1
else	Who else? 28/1
embassy	The Fair bus stops right over there, in front of the embassy. 30/1
enemy	So I made an enemy. 31/1
engine	He loves following fire engines. 32/1
enough	It's large enough, and modern and businesslike. 28/2
entrance	They kept taking pictures of the bank entrance. 32/2
especially	Eighty-eighth Street is usually a busy street, especially during the summer. 34/1
essay	He wanted to work on a photographic essay on bonsai. 29/2
estate	I could be a real estate agent, a travel agent, anything, as long as it isn't boring. 29/3
event	The magazine sent them all over the world to cover important events. 29/2
exactly	No. It wasn't exactly Pedro's fault, but Michael wouldn't speak to him after that. 31/2
experience	She decided she wanted to write a book about her experiences at the magazine. 29/2
fallen	Pedro has fallen in love many times, hasn't he? 33/2
fast	You give up too fast. 28/1
favor	Would you do me a favor? 30/1
felt	I felt uncomfortable there. 28/2
figure	I'm just figuring something out. 31/1
finger	I cut my finger, and I couldn't stop the bleeding. 31/1
finish	We won't announce the contest until Mr. Crawford finishes the brochure. 28/2
fireman	When I grow up, I want to be a fireman like my father. 32/2
fit	His office is large enough for twenty people to fit in. 28/2
forgive	Yes, but now that Michael is seeing Joana, I hope he'll forgive Pedro. 31/2
forgotten	Michael hasn't forgotten the whole thing, has he? 33/2
forth	They kept walking back and forth in front of the bank. 32/2
frequently	Michael changes jobs more frequently than anyone I know. 28/1
friendship	I know, but I think a good friendship deserves a second chance. 31/2
gain	I know I shouldn't gain any more weight, but I still love to eat dessert. 30/1
given	Michael hasn't given himself a deadline, has he? 33/2
gotten	You've gotten thinner since August. 33/1

graduate   I couldn't type when I graduated from high school, but I can now.   27/1

grateful   I am impressed, Sergeant, impressed and grateful.   32/2

groceries   A couple was passing by and helped me pick up my groceries. 31/1

grown   You've grown a beard since you quit your job.   33/1

guard   On June 5, at exactly 2:20, when two of the four guards were out to lunch, the three suspects moved toward the entrance of the bank.   34/2

gun   When they got up to the tellers, they took guns out of paper bags.   34/2

heart   Pedro has broken a lot of hearts, hasn't he?   33/2

heat   There's never any heat.   28/2

hero   You are his hero.   32/1

hope   Yes, but now that Michael is seeing Joana, I hope he'll forgive Pedro.   31/2

host   You're a great host.   27/1

hostess   Well, you're a pretty good hostess.   27/1

house   They all have good jobs and houses in the country.   29/3

immediately   In fact, we're starting the project immediately.   28/1

impressed   I am impressed, Sergeant, impressed and grateful.   32/2

in charge   And guess who's in charge?   28/1

insist   He insists on pretending to be you, Sergeant.   32/1

interested   They weren't interested.   28/1

journalist   The woman is a journalist.   29/2

judge   We won't announce the contest until my boss chooses the judges.   28/2

jump   Children run, and jump, and fall.   34/1

keep in touch Haven't you kept in touch?   33/1

kept   He kept to himself a lot.   29/1

known   They've known each other for a month.   33/1

lately   Pedro has done a lot of new things lately, hasn't he?   33/2

laugh   They laugh, happy to see each other.   34/1

lecture   Hey, I didn't ask for a lecture!   28/1

lie   My father says I shouldn't tell so many lies.   30/1

linguistics   Are you still interested in linguistics?   33/2

liquor   It still makes me happy to see the liquor bottles beside the old French mirror.   34/3

literature   Are you still interested in literature?   33/2

local   When there are local tragedies, they are there, too.   29/2

lose   How is he going to lose weight?   28/2

loud   Michael talks louder than anyone I know.   28/1

low   This shelf is low enough for Ali to reach.   28/2

mark   They kept marking things down on a yellow pad.   32/2

master   Does he have to paint as well as the masters?   28/2

meal   I used to live from meal to meal.   27/2

meanwhile	Meanwhile, the other non-uniformed policemen arrived. 34/2
measure	How is he going to measure success? 28/2
medal	They won many awards and medals. 29/2
medicine	Are you still interested in medicine? 33/2
men	He's one of our undercover men. 32/1
mirror	It still makes me happy to see the liquor bottles beside the old French mirror. 34/3
moment	Now they are ready to go, day or night, on a moment's notice. 29/2
morning	I can do it by myself in the morning. 27/1
movement	We needed more proof, so I started noting their movements carefully. 32/2
myself	I can do it by myself in the morning. 27/1
nearby	He mentioned that he lived nearby as we were walking home. 31/1
nose	Hussein pinched Ali right under his father's nose. 32/2
note	We needed more proof, so I started noting their movements carefully. 32/2
notify	Why did you wait for three days before notifying the police? 32/2
obvious	They were trying to look and act like tourists, but they obviously were not. 34/2
old-fashioned	I know it's old-fashioned, but that's what I like about it. 34/3
opposite	The Fair bus stops right over there, directly opposite the Japanese Garden. 30/1
paid	We haven't paid the bill, have we? 33/2
patience	I don't have the patience. 29/3
pavement	The groceries spilled all over the pavement. 31/1
person	The house is too big for one person to live in. 27/2
personal	I'd like to thank him personally. 32/1
pickpocket	How did you find out those three were pickpockets? 32/2
pinch	Hussein pinched Ali right under his father's nose. 32/2
place	Every place I see him, he's with a different woman. 31/2
pleasant	His office looks very spacious and pleasant. 28/2
police	Why did you wait for three days before notifying the police? 32/2
policeman	The policeman sold ice cream right under the robbers' noses. 32/2
polite	He says it's not polite. 30/1
pool	You've swum in the Crawfords' pool, haven't you? 33/2
position	Many other magazines and newspapers offered them positions, but at this point the man and the woman decided to work independently. 29/2
pretend	He's eighteen months older than I am, but as kids we used to wear the same clothes and pretend we were twins! 29/1

professional   They enjoyed their work and grew professionally.   29/2

progress   We haven't made a lot of progress, have we?   33/2

project   In fact, we're starting the project immediately.   28/1

proof   We needed more proof, so I started noting their movements carefully.   32/2

prove   But he has to prove something to himself.   28/2

push   Parents push baby carriages.   34/1

quick   You even eat more quickly than you used to.   28/1

quite   It's quite a long walk from here.   30/1

reach   This shelf is low enough for Ali to reach.   28/2

recent   Michael hasn't drunk any beer recently, has he?   33/2

record   When I was a teenager, I used to listen to records.   27/2

regular   Do you come here regularly?   30/2

respect   When they go out into the street, no one asks for their autographs, but everyone in their profession knows and respects them.   29/2

robber   The policeman sold ice cream right under the robbers' noses.   32/2

robbery   There was a robbery at Dad's bank!   32/2

rug   I can vacuum the rugs later.   27/1

safe   It's not safe to walk in the park at night.   30/1

sat   At noon on June 3, three men bought sandwiches and ice cream, and sat on one of the benches in front of the International Bank.   34/2

seen   I haven't seen her for almost three years.   33/1

sensitive   Well, Michael is sensitive.   31/2

separate   When they finished their separate projects, they decided to work as a team again.   29/2

settle   Now that Michael is seeing Joana, I hope he and Pedro will settle their differences.   31/2

sew   I like to sew.   29/3

share   They don't seem to share many interests.   31/2

shelf   This shelf is low enough for Ali to reach.   28/2

shoplifter   How did you guess those three were shoplifters?   32/2

should   You should take the Fair bus.   30/1

sidewalk   My packages spilled all over the sidewalk.   31/1

since   Much better since I spoke to you last.   33/1

sing   Yes, he sings badly.   28/1

single   I couldn't change diapers when I was single, but I can now.   27/1

ski   I don't know how to ski.   32/1

sleep   Paulo sleeps less than anyone I know.   28/1

slept   We haven't slept late all week, have we?   33/2

slip   I slipped and almost fell while I was walking home.   31/1

slow   Michael eats more slowly than anyone I know.   28/1

solve	He loves trying to solve crimes.	32/1
soon	You give up sooner than you used to.	28/1
spacious	His office looks very spacious and pleasant.	28/2
spell	Michael spells worse than anyone I know.	28/1
spill	My packages spilled all over the sidewalk.	31/1
spin	My head is spinning.	29/3
spoken	I haven't spoken to Michael in three years.	33/1
stairs	As I was walking down the stairs, I tripped and fell.	31/1
step	Then each one takes a few steps, turns, and waves good-bye. 34/1	
stole	The customer stole a watch right under the salesman's nose. 32/2	
stood	One of the suspects stood at the door of the bank.	34/2
straighten	I hurt my back, and I couldn't straighten up.	31/1
success	How is he going to measure success?	28/2
successful	He wants to paint as successfully as the masters.	28/2
suit	This suit is formal enough for Paulo to wear to the party. 28/2	
surprised	I am surprised, Sergeant, surprised and delighted.	32/2
suspect	I suspected something right away.	32/2
suspicious	Why did you wait for three days before getting suspicious? 32/2	
swim	Yes, he swims fast.	28/1
swum	You've swum in the Crawford's pool, haven't you?	33/2
taken	I haven't taken a day off for a week.	33/1
teenager	You know, when I was a teenager, I used to go to parties all the time.	27/2
teller	When they got up to the tellers, they took guns out of paper bags.	34/2
thankful	I am amazed, Sergeant, amazed and thankful.	32/2
thieves	Captain, would you tell me who is responsible for catching the thieves?	32/1
through	I could see this through the windows of the bank.	34/2
tongue	I burned my tongue, and I couldn't taste the food.	31/1
tourist	They kept trying to look and act like tourists.	32/2
toward	Two women, both lost in thought, walk toward each other. 34/1	
tragedy	When there are local tragedies, they are there, too.	29/2
travel	I was tired of travelling by myself.	27/1
trip	One day while I was coming down 88th Street, I tripped and fell.	31/1
twin	He's eighteen months older than I am, but as kids we used to wear the same clothes and pretend we were twins!	29/1
twist	I twisted my ankle, and I couldn't stand up.	31/1

typewriter   I'd rather work with people than with files and typewriters. 29/3

uncomfortable   I felt uncomfortable there.   28/2

undercover   He's one of our undercover men.   32/1

urge   I urge you not to talk about this.   32/1

used to   You know, when I was a teenager, I used to go to parties all the time.   27/2

vacuum   I can vacuum the rugs later.   27/1

warn   I must warn you not to talk about this.   32/1

wash   I can do a wash later.   27/1

waste   My father says I shouldn't waste so much time.   30/1

wave   Then each one takes a few steps, turns, and waves good-bye. 34/1

whenever   Whenever I see him, he's with a different woman.   31/2

wherever   Wherever I see him, he's with a different woman.   31/2

whole   Let's have a beer and forget the whole thing.   33/2

won   They won many awards and medals.   29/2

worn   I haven't worn a suit for ages.   33/1

worse   Michael spells worse than anyone I know.   28/1

wrist   I broke my wrist, and I couldn't move my fingers.   31/1

written   I haven't written home in a couple of days.   33/1